Can I Get A Ruling?

Golf Rules Revealed Through Others' Mistakes

DAVE MARRANDETTE

CLOCK
TOWER
PRESS

For information address   Clock Tower Press
                          3622 W. Liberty Rd.
                          Ann Arbor, MI 48103
                          www.clocktowerpress.com

Illustrations by Bruce Worden
Cover Design by Marty Somberg

Library of Congress Cataloging-in-Publication Data:

          Marrandette, David G., 1947-
          Can I get a ruling? : golf rules revealed through others' mistakes / Dave Marrandette.
          p. cm.
          Includes bibliographical references.
          ISBN 1-932202-21-8
          1. Golf—Rules. 2. Golf—Anecdotes. I. Title.
          GV971.M37 2004
          796.352'02'022—dc22
          2004016319

CONTENTS

A Guide to the Book

If you play golf long enough, even if you're a casual player who ventures out to the links but once or twice a year, you will, in some manner, in some place, encounter the rules of golf. Whether it's during the course of playing the game or whether it's through a situation after the fact, you will surely have the opportunity to open, or at least be subject to, the rulebook. If you watch golf on television or as a spectator at a live event, you will likely witness a rules situation. Whatever the circumstances of your encounter, you will probably come to the conclusion that, while the rules of golf are intended to be fair, they will at times seem imperfect, illogical or quirky.

As you read through this book, you will discover actual situations where a particular rule or rules have been applied. Most of the cases are from professional tournaments—the PGA, LPGA or European Tours. It's obvious why. As you might expect, you will find many references to incidents that have occurred during major championships. This is due to the magnitude of the event and also the heightened publicity that follows. It is astounding how many rule incidents have had a direct effect on the outcome of major championships. In a few instances, a real-life, non-professional incident is brought to light. Conversely, there are hundreds of incidents that occur annually in competitive golf that go unpublicized or perhaps unnoticed. The discovery of some of these was exciting and challenging and their inclusion makes this book unique.

Many of the situations chronicled here are recent, occurring within the last 50 years. That's partly due to the timing of this book, but mostly due to the medium of television. Let's face it—it's a lot easier to keep up with the golf happenings in today's electronic world. Many golf tournaments are broadcasted on television. In addition to television the Internet and the print media are very informative.

There are some circumstances that are recounted from the past, some distant and some not so distant. You may notice that some of these cases involve a rule that is different from what we know it as today. The rules have evolved throughout the years and every effort was made to point out any differences between then and now. However, this is not intended to be an examination of the history of the rules. When you encounter situations where the rules at the time of the case in question differ from what the rules are today, this is where you will come upon a brief history of the rules. Occasionally I have injected a brief sentence or two concerning the origin or historic detail of a particular rule or a specific point in the rules. An excellent discourse on the history of the rules is Kenneth G. Chapman's work *The Rules of the Green—A History of the Rules of Golf*. Be aware that the rules have changed greatly since the first code was put on parchment in 1744. The rules from that period in the history of golf had their emphasis on match play, the dominant, and virtually only, form of the game. As you study the cases here, be aware that the decisions made or penalties assessed were based on what the rulebook stated at that time. The rules have continued to evolve in the more than 260 years since that first code was written. In almost all cases you will notice how the rules have become increasingly complex in comparison to the original 13.

Gentleman Golfers of Leith 1744—Rules of Golf

I. You must Tee your Ball within a Club length of the Hole.

II. Your Tee must be upon the ground.

III. You are not to change the Ball which you strike off the Tee.

IV. You are not to remove Stones, Bones, or any Break-club for the sake of playing your Ball, except upon the fair Green, and that only within a Club length of your Ball.

V. If your Ball come among Water, or any watery filth, you are at liberty to take out your Ball, and bringing it behind the hazard, and teeing it, you may play it with any club and allow your Adversary a stroke for so getting out your Ball.

VI. If your Balls be found anywhere touching one another, you are to lift the first Ball till you play the last.

VII. At holing, you are to play your Ball honestly for the Hole, and not play upon your Adversary's Ball, not lying in your way to the Hole.

VIII. If you should lose your Ball by its being taken up, or in any other way, you are to go back to the spot where you struck last, and drop another Ball, and allow your Adversary a stroke for your misfortune.

IX. No man, at Holing his Ball, is to be allowed to mark to the Hole with his Club or anything else.

X. If a Ball be stop'd by any person, Horse, Dog, or anything else, the Ball so stop'd must be played where it lyes.

XI. If you draw your Club in order to strike, and proceed as far in the stroke as to be bringing down your Club—if then your Club shall break in any way, it is to be accounted a stroke.

XII. He whose Ball lyes farthest from the Hole is obliged to play first.

XIII. Neither Trench, Ditch, nor Dyke made for the preservation of the Links, nor the Scholars' holes, nor the Soldiers' lines, shall be accounted a Hazard, but the Ball is to be taken out, Teed, and played with any iron Club.

This will not be a walk through the rulebook, a rule-by-rule examination and a real case for every rule. That would be boring, tedious and quite common. I have selected entertaining and enlightening situations that will stir the reader's interest in the rules of golf and provide a bit of human interest along the way. Additionally, I will not try to explain or interpret the rules. There are many volumes available that provide clarification of each rule, many giving hypothetical examples to explain the proper procedures. Instead, I have uniquely categorized the situations, using appropriate themes to divide the sections. To cover interpretation of the rules, I have included a section on Rules Officials and Interpretation.

In many illustrations more than one rule is applicable to a particular situation. I have taken great care to place each "multiple" situation in its appropriate category, using the predominant theme of the case. For instance, the issue of time is always involved in the search for and identification of a ball that is potentially lost. Thus, when the five-minute time limit is the central focus, that case is placed in the chapter on Time. If the emphasis of the circumstances focused on other factors, such as identification of the ball, then that case was put in the appropriate chapter. This task was challenging at times, but each chapter is reflective of what is contained in it.

Occasionally (although it often seems frequently) a rule infraction is not discovered until after the player has completed his round and signed his scorecard. In these cases, if a player has been assessed a penalty because of a violation, he will already have signed an incorrect scorecard and thus be disqualified. I have viewed these circumstances differently than situations where a player either forgets to sign his scorecard or signs for an incorrect score due to human error or oversight.

Golf is a game of chance and therefore luck (termed "rub of the green" in the rulebook) is an integral part of the game. You will see how the element of luck plays a part in several of the cases described here. The modern golfer has tried to dismiss luck from the game. It cannot be done. Our golfing forefathers realized that luck was a fundamental element of the game and accepted it as part of the mental challenge as well as allowing for it in the rulebook.

This examination of rule incidents should prove to be educational. At the very least, every player will become aware of the intricacies of the rules. Keep a rulebook handy as you read through this material. It will help you to understand a particular rule if you refer to it while studying the situation. By all means, enjoy it. It is intended to be entertaining as well as educational.

Introduction

In its basic concept, golf is no different than any other sport. It is a game with a set of rules that participants must follow when playing. Any deviation from or infraction of one or more of the rules produces a penalty. In golf it's one stroke, two strokes, four strokes, one hole, two holes or disqualification. Yet, ironically, what sets golf apart from other sports are its rules. The rules of golf are central to the game. They include a succinct yet complex code that is intended to be followed by all players. Since the playing field is so vast, each player is virtually at all times "on his honor" to observe the rules. The rules have been developed to insure that all participants play the same game. They have also been created to inform the player of his rights and procedures in virtually any situation that he may encounter.

Having a thorough and working knowledge of the rules can be a tremendous benefit for not only the touring professional, but also for the everyday recreational golfer. Understanding the rules and being able to properly apply them will often save a player one or more strokes during a round. Golf is not only a physical sport that demands the ultimate in hand-to-eye coordination, but it is also a thinking man's sport both in the strategy involved in playing the game and in the ability to apply the rules as the game progresses. More than any other sport, golf combines the physical and the mental, and the rules are an essential part of the mental side of the game.

The application of the rules allows for imaginative interpretation. In other sports, application of the rules involves the judgment of an official for virtually every play or situation. In golf—most of the time—the application involves interpretation by the player alone or a rules official. The rules of golf are assembled in a small volume entitled *The Rules of Golf*, published by the United States Golf Association (USGA) for play in the United States, its territories and Mexico and by the Royal and Ancient Golf Club for play everywhere else in the world. These two self-appointed ruling bodies of the game also interpret various rule situations as they occur. These interpretations are updated and published yearly in a hefty volume known as the "Decisions on the Rules of Golf." This publication further explains each rule in light of the various circumstances that have occurred and the decisions resulting from them.

Not many of us are intimately familiar with that small book, let alone the complete decision book. We might think we are, but, if we are honest with ourselves, we really do not have a working knowledge of the rules (if you doubt this statement, try taking one of the many rules quizzes on the Internet or in any golf magazine). Round after round, year after year, the majority of us play our own version of the game, slightly modifying the rules to adjust for conditions or our needs. The "rules" the average amateur follows in day-to-day play are frequently different from those adhered to by the ladies and gentlemen of professional and high-caliber amateur golf. This is partly due to circumstances and partly due to self-imposed indulgence.

In reality we modify the rules to suit the conditions of our play. How many of us strictly adhere to Rule 18 (Ball at Rest Moved)? Then, do we revert to Rule 20.3(D) when the ball fails to remain on its original spot? This is not necessarily wrong. You don't have to do much research to prove that "we" outnumber "them" by a large margin. We play a totally different game under vastly different conditions. We epitomize the way the game is really played. All of the rules of golf and the resulting decisions are needed for professional or top-notch amateur golf. Competition at that level requires a precise code of rules. For the amount of money and prestige professionals play for, no situation should go unchecked. However, daily golf in the amateur world appears to follow a much different set of rules.

But should it? Are precise measurements and exact drop spots needed? Must we modify the rules for expedience of play? The answers to these questions are No-Yes-No. One of the most intriguing aspects of golf is that by playing by the same set of rules, the worst amateur can measure his ability against the top professional. He could even compete on a "level" playing field by utilizing the USGA handicap system. The average player is able to compete on the same "field of play" as the best professional in the world, but he will only be able to accurately compare his ability if he plays by the same set of rules. If he modifies the rules to suit his circumstances, the comparison becomes imprecise and the enjoyment becomes diminished. Adherence to the rules helps every player take pleasure in participation in the game.

The rules of golf reflect the spirit of the game. The game itself was being played long before the first code of rules was published. The etiquette and spirit of the game are exhibited in that first set of rules and have been maintained ever since. Honesty and integrity, the hallmarks of the game, echo throughout every rulebook ever published. It is these virtues that set golf apart from all other sports. In no other sport are players expected to police themselves concerning the rules. Every time he plays, each player tests not only the level of his physical ability, but also the level of his honesty and integrity. Golf is the ultimate test of character. It's no wonder that corporations will frequently evaluate potential employees on the golf course, observing how they handle the mental and emotional aspects of the game.

The structure of the rulebook is such that it is relatively easy to locate a rule if one takes just a little time to familiarize himself with it. There are three major sections to the book: I. Etiquette, II. Definitions and III. Rules of Play. Unfortunately, Sections I & II, which generate the foundation for the actual rules, are generally overlooked by the golfing masses. Section III contains 11 subsections breaking down the rules into subject categories. If you think the rules of golf can get quite complicated and cumbersome, consider this: Before 1984 there were 41 rules in the book in contrast to the 34 that there are today.

The number of rules and the fact that each player has a different knowledge level concerning them does not change the reality that the rules are meant to be followed by everyone. They exist not only as instruction for participation, but also as a guide to the spirit of golf.

ETIQUETTE

While breaches of etiquette are not penalized in the modern game, they certainly are in bad taste and reflect poor sportsmanship in a game that is the epitome of honorable competition. Although etiquette was not an "official" part of the rules that affected the play of the competition until 2004, it has always been of vital importance for the enjoyment of the game.

With the changes in the rules that occurred in 2004, etiquette has now been reestablished as a meaningful part of the game. First, the section on Etiquette in *The Rules of Golf*—which not coincidentally happens to be Section I—has been strengthened with double the number of pages from the previous version. It has been revised and amplified to provide a player with more guidance concerning his conduct on the golf course. Second, the committee conducting a golf competition now has the authority to disqualify any player in the case of a serious breach of Etiquette. Slowly, the decorum of the game is being restored.

The snapshots that follow indicate how proper etiquette or the lack of it can possibly affect the outcome of an event.

Sam Snead was no doubt one of the sweetest swingers the game has ever seen. He was enormously successful, winning three Masters, three PGAs and one British Open. But he was snake bit in the U.S. Open, and none more so than the 1947 U.S. Open at St. Louis Country Club.

After 72 holes of regulation play Snead had worked himself into a play-off with Lew Worsham. In the playoff on the following day, when the players reached the area around the 18th green, they were all even. Worsham chipped from the fringe to about three feet and Snead's downhill 20-footer stopped short approximately the same distance. Snead stepped to his ball to make his putt, but Worsham halted him, asking if he was sure he was away. A

USGA rules official came to the scene and informed Snead that the rules stated whoever was away putted first. A measurement was taken and found that Snead was indeed away—by one

inch. But the ploy had worked. Snead, rattled by the incident, missed the putt. Worsham made and won the championship. Was it the rules of etiquette or gamesmanship?

The British Open of 1876 had a most fascinating conclusion resulting from what we would consider today a breach of etiquette. At that time it was a violation of the rules.

David Strath, a runner-up in both the 1870 and 1872 British Opens, and Robert Martin, one of the premier players of the day, tied at the end of regulation play with scores of 176 (the tournament was 36 holes back then). But before a playoff could be arranged, a complaint was entered against Strath claiming that he had broken the rules by hitting his approach to the 17th green while the players ahead were still putting, allegedly striking one of them (at that time, this action was against the rules). To further compound the matter, the players were not British Open participants.

In the formative days of the Open, which began at Prestwick (Scotland) in 1860, the organization and administration of the tournament were quite casual, even to the extent that the course itself was not set aside strictly for the play of the championship. Thus the competitors mingled in with the local golfers out for a casual game of their own.

Strath, an overtly-defensive type, became disgruntled with the complaint itself and the amount of time consumed by the tournament committee to decide the issue. He bluntly refused a playoff and Martin was declared the winner by default—but only after he himself had walked the course to make the result official in strict accordance with the rules.

HONESTY

It is often stated how great the game of golf is. But what is it that sets golf apart from all other sports, whether they are team or individual? What is it that makes the game so appealing to everyone, men and women, young and old, skilled and unskilled?

Golf is the one major sport where true sportsmanship and gentlemanly conduct still exist. The integrity of the golfer is just as important today as it was 300 years ago. It must be that way, for golf is the only sport where players must regulate themselves. Because of the extreme size of the playing field and the overwhelming manpower issue and logistics that would be involved, it is impossible to monitor each player's every action. Except in major championships, there are no referees who follow a player's every move to indicate fouls or infractions or lend assistance. Moreover, it is the sole remaining sport where rule infractions are not looked at with a wink of the eye. At a time when the Roman gladiator attitude has overcome all other sports, golf remains alone with sportsmanship at its base.

Other major spectator sports, whether they are team or individually oriented, have lost the true sportsman. They have degenerated to the point where fights, temper tantrums or illegal actions are now the accepted standard within the competition. Hockey is notorious for its recurring fights. If you attend a hockey game and no fight occurs, you feel slighted—at least a little bit. You didn't get your money's worth. The old adage, "I went to a fight the other night and a hockey game broke out," speaks more truth than jovial fiction. While it's true that hockey is a high-speed, contact sport, once a player feels his pride has been damaged, he drops the stick, discards the gloves and commences to defend his honor. Standing-room-only is often the ticket for the penalty box. Much talk is generated about curbing the violence and the fights.

"Stiff" fines and penalties have been instituted. This hardly seems to discourage an offended player.

Football is also a violent, contact sport, even more so than hockey. Players try to get away with whatever illegal actions they can. Grudges, with revenge as the final solution, are held from game-to-game, season-to-season, and even throughout careers. Retirement or confrontation is the only way to resolve the difference. Like hockey, the football hierarchy is trying to crack down on violence with the game. For excessive violence, players are slapped with a fine that hardly dents the wallet. Occasionally their crime results in a more serious penalty: suspension for a game or two.

Baseball, while considerably less violent than football or hockey, still enjoys an occasional, old-fashioned, bench-clearing brawl or a rush to the pitcher's mound by an offended batter. Temper tantrums by high-spirited managers are increasingly commonplace. Pitchers take the liberty of "doctoring" the ball. Some argue that it's the tradition of the game. Hogwash! Poor sportsmanship and cheating have no place in any sports competition.

In recent years basketball has experienced an ever-growing number of altercations between players. Anyone who thinks basketball is a non-contact sport has probably been in a coma for the past 20 to 30 years. Many fouls are more than just a bump or whack on the arm. Television announcers call this a "hard takedown." No kidding. What sport is this? Wrestling? Coaches are a tyrannical lot. Whenever you see a coach up on the sidelines and shouting onto the floor, you can bet he's not always exhorting his players to a more exemplary performance.

The supreme crybaby sport was and occasionally still is tennis. One questionable call by a linesman or a net judge will often send a player into a fit of rage, frequently insulting the ability or parentage of the official. Fines or suspensions are levied, but never seem to alter the future behavior of the offender. It is precisely for this reason—lack of sportsmanship and gentlemanly conduct—that tennis has experienced a decline during the past two decades. John McEnroe's behavior was hardly role-model worthy.

Golf, on the other hand, has a totally different atmosphere and attitude about sportsmanship and fair play. While golf does not contain the element of physical contact that provokes outrage, sportsmanship is an integral part of the game. Strict adherence to the rules maintains the integrity of the sport. In no other sporting competition do players invoke penalties on themselves for unseen infractions of the rules.

Professional golfers play for huge amounts of money. One stroke can mean the difference of hundreds of thousands of dollars. This is the source of their livelihood. There are no guaranteed salaries. Yet it is the accepted and expected practice for a player to invoke a penalty on himself despite the fact that the infraction was unseen by anyone else.

A player would never think of throwing a temper tantrum after receiving an unfavorable ruling from a tournament official. His reputation and credibility would be destroyed, not to mention the disciplinary action and the pinch on his pocketbook that would follow.

Golfers know the traditions and honor of their sport. If they inadvertently break a rule and it is brought to their attention, they accept the consequences, regardless of the timing. The history of tournament competition is littered with examples of players who have been disqualified after the fact. While a disqualification due to an unknown rules violation is never pleasant, it is accepted in respect to the honor and tradition of the game.

Strict adherence to the rules maintains the integrity of the sport. Tradition, honor and pride have everything to do with the trustworthiness of the game.

To aptly demonstrate the above-mentioned point, LPGA touring professional Wendy Ward is an excellent case to examine. Her honesty and integrity were tested not once, but twice within a month's time.

During the final round of the 2000 LPGA Championship, Ward, a former U.S. Amateur champion (1994), was in the heat of the battle. As she prepared to putt on the 13th green she addressed her ball, grounded her putter and then abruptly backed away. "My ball has moved," she exclaimed.

The rules official following the group quickly rushed to her side to sort out the situation. Ward explained that the ball had turned ever so slightly. "I know exactly how I set my ball when I putt. On a Callaway ball, its imprint, 'Rule 35,' stares right at me. It moved." It never crossed her mind that in the process of replacing her ball she may have misaligned it.

The instant replay of the television cameras immediately set into motion. Several attempts to detect the movement of the ball were unsuccessful. But Ward knew the ball had moved and she had no option but to assess herself a one-stroke penalty. Rule 18.2(B) decrees that "if a player's ball moves after he has addressed it, the player shall be deemed to have moved the ball and shall incur a penalty stroke."

The stoke penalty prevented Ward from a tie for first place in the championship and participating in a playoff with Julie Inkster and Italy's Stefania Croce and a chance at the first-place check of $210,000. Her third-place finish gave her a payday of $76,319.

Eventual champion Juli Inkster, her playing partner that day, said of

Ward's actions, "No one would have known. To do what she did shows true integrity. She is the real champion today."

Almost unbelievably, she had encountered the same situation three weeks earlier during an LPGA event in Rochester, New York. She had taken the same action then.

———————

Rule 5 and its associated Appendix III provide guidance concerning the condition of the golf ball and its specifications. High-level competition such as the PGA Tour places stringent requirements on the balls that are used. Even though the ball may conform to USGA specifications, it may still be impermissible for play.

During the 1996 Greater Hartford Open at the TPC at River Highlands in Cromwell, Connecticut, Greg Norman shot six-under in the first round to tie for the lead and then slipped to fourth place with a three-over 73 in the second round. But Norman disqualified himself before the start of the third round because he had been using a ball that was improperly stamped. This may seem to be a minuscule and confusing point to the average golfer, but not to Norman. While the Maxfli ball that Norman was testing conformed to USGA specifications, it did not have the official side stamp reference.

"The ball was stamped wrong," Norman explained. "There was nothing illegal about the ball I've been using. Yesterday, Maxfli informed me of this situation and in accordance with the rules of golf, I have no choice but to disqualify myself. You live by the rules of golf. I didn't understand the rule."

Ben Nelson, PGA Tour Tournament Director, commented, "It seems so minute, but that's the way they can control what golf balls are played within competition."

———————

Here's a situation that we could have included in any one of three sections—Knowledge, On the Green or Honesty. We chose to include it here because of the impeccable reputation of Tom Kite.

During the 1995 U.S. Open played at Shinnecock Hills on Long Island, New York, Kite faced a one-foot putt for a bogey-five on the final green of the third round. He addressed the putt and tapped it in, but not before briefly stepping away and then readdressing the putt. Before he signed his scorecard, he reported to the referee that he believed his ball had moved after he addressed it. Since he had not replaced the ball he incurred a two-stroke penalty, turning his bogey-five into a triple-bogey seven.

As a further example of Kite's irreproachable honesty and to show how meticulous one must be when taking relief, we relate the following incident.

During the third round of the 1993 Kemper Open at the TPC at Avenel in Potomac, Maryland, Kite was leading and playing with his closest pursuer, New Zealander Grant Waite. Waite's second shot on the par-4 fourth missed the green and finished in an area designated as ground-under-repair. Waite took relief and was preparing to hit his pitch shot when Kite glanced over and noticed that one of his heels was inside the ground-under-repair area. If Waite hit the shot, he would be penalized two strokes for failure to take complete relief (Rule 25.1(B)(1)). It would have been easy for Kite to "overlook"

the infraction until after Waite had played. His lead would have increased by two strokes immediately. But Kite spoke up. "We don't need any penalties here," said Kite, gesturing toward Waite's feet. Waite looked down and realized his mistake, redropped and finished the hole.

The next day Waite won by a shot. Kite finished second.

"What goes around comes around" is usually associated with actions in a negative context. However, it can also be applied to positive or honest actions. Every golf fan is familiar with the dramatic rise of Ben Curtis to the top of the golf echelon. Before Curtis became the 2003 British Open Champion he had to endure the rigors and pressure of Qualifying School just like every other PGA Tour hopeful. In the 2000 event he displayed the character that would eventually elevate him to the 2003 British Open Championship.

At the completion of the second round during phase two of the 2000 qualifying tournament, Curtis was in excellent position to earn his card for the 2001 PGA Tour season. However, in the course of conversation at dinner following that round, Curtis learned that he had taken an incorrect drop from casual water.

Without a further word to anyone, the next day Curtis reported the infraction to tournament officials. The result, of course, was disqualification and another year of grinding it out on the mini-tours. But the black cloud of that day, as we all know, had a silver lining.

Here are two related incidents that demonstrate that a little honesty goes a long way. In both cases the ruling that was rendered was a direct result of actions by the same player. The exact thought process of this player is difficult to determine. Read the cases and make your own judgment.

In the spring of 2003, Brandel Chamblee had completed his second round of the Chrysler Classic of Tucson with a fine 65 that put him in a tie for third place. His card had been kept by Marco Dawson who, by signing the card, had attested that the score on each and every hole was correct. But after signing the card, Dawson questioned the drop Chamblee had taken on the 16th hole. In question were Rules 25.2 and 20.2(C)(1.F), which state that if a ball rolls more than two club-lengths after it is dropped, it must be redropped. Chamblee had taken a drop from an embedded lie on a mound. On the first drop the ball rolled down the slope, considerably more than two club-lengths from where it initially touched the ground. But on the second drop, it was difficult to determine just how far the ball had rolled, certainly more than one but maybe less than two club-lengths. Chamblee, thinking that the rule prescribed one club-length, retrieved the ball and placed it on the spot where the ball hit the ground and played away.

Dawson might never have thought further about the incident if his wife had not made a comment about the drop as they were leaving the golf course. She simply inquired why Chamblee had measured one club-length instead of two. This got Dawson thinking, but instead of contacting PGA Tour officials on site, Dawson called an official on the Nationwide Tour to confirm the rule. The Nationwide Tour official then called PGA officials in Tucson. They in turn contacted Chamblee to confirm the details of the situation. Indeed, a violation had occurred and Chamblee had to be assessed a two-stroke penalty. Because he had already signed his card, he was disqualified.

Now fast forward to the 2003 Disney tournament conducted at Disney World just outside of Orlando, Florida. Once again Marco Dawson was at the center of a controversy involving a situation in which a ball was dropped. This time the sufferer was Esteban Toledo, Dawson's playing partner.

On the last hole of the second round on the Palm Course, Toledo hit his ball into an area marked as ground-under-repair that permitted him to drop at the closest point of relief. Toledo's closest point of relief was to the left, but he chose to drop to the right. From there he played on to the green and finished with a 66, good enough to make the cut by one shot.

Once again, Dawson signed the card. But later, when he was reviewing the round, he thought the drop made by Toledo was "unusual." The next day he went out to the spot and contacted a rules official. The final ruling was made on Sunday morning. Toledo was assessed a two-stroke penalty and then disqualified for signing an incorrect scorecard.

Dawson claimed that he never actually saw Toledo take the drop and that no rules official was called to the spot to assist. He just assumed Toledo knew what he was doing. Dawson excused his actions by stating, "The only question I had is whether my knowledge of the rules was as good as it should have been." Even during a conversation with Toledo following the incident, Dawson was unapologetic. His final statement, "What's more important? Your image or doing the right thing?"

Here's an incident that you might expect to find under our Caddy section. However, we chose to place it here because it serves to illustrate the honor of the caddies on the professional tours. While their livelihood is dependent on their player's score and their existence seems a bit nomadic, they still uphold the backbone of the game—integrity. All players are looking for a caddy with this trait.

Australian Peter Lonard has steadily ascended the ladder of the world rankings. An invitation to the WGC-Accenture Match Play Championship means you are in the top 64 in the world. During the 2003 event, Lonard lost in the semifinals and then faced fellow Australian Adam Scott in the third-place match. Lonard lost the first two holes of the match and on the third, he went for the green in two on the par-5. He hooked the ball to the left of the green and it finished in some tall grass. Before Lonard and his caddy Ken Herring arrived at the scene, a small army of marshals had already begun the search. As Lonard and Herring searched, Herring suddenly felt something under his foot. When he looked down and saw his player's ball, he knew exactly what to do. A rules official was summoned and Lonard was instructed to replace the ball where Herring had seen it and take a one-stroke penalty. Lonard made a miraculous pitch to six feet and made the putt for par to tie Scott. Lonard eventually made a comeback, but lost the match one down to Scott. The consequences of that third hole may have cost him $90,000, the difference between third and fourth place. "I'm just glad he piped up and said he did it," said Lonard. "A lot of people might not have said anything."

———————

The concluding two incidents well delineate why golf is such a great game in developing positive character traits. As has been made evident by this chapter, honesty is one of the fundamental building blocks of the game. Youngsters who take up the game constantly hear such a speech. But those words must be followed by the proper actions to have any significant and lasting meaning. It is incumbent on those who play, teach, coach or in any way mentor someone who plays the game to set a positive example.

This first incident introduces us to a high school golf coach who practices what he preaches. The precise details of the proceedings are far less significant than the actions of the coach.

In October of 2002, the Westborough, Massachusetts High School golf team competed in the Division II State Team Championships. At the end of the event it appeared that they had captured their first state golf title since 1965, winning in a tiebreaker based on the fifth-place score. Celebrations ensued and plaques were awarded.

Then, tragically, there was a reversal of fortunes. Greg Rota, Westborough High School golf coach, is a meticulous individual. At the conclusion of every match Rota placed all the scores in his computer for record keeping and eventual evaluation. As he was posting the scores, Rota became aware that one of his player's cards was incorrect. The player had taken a nine instead of a seven on the final hole. Since the scorecard had already been signed, the result, of course, meant disqualification for that player. With the disqualification, Westborough would have to revert to another player's score and lose the championship by three shots. Rota knew what had to be done. He quickly notified officials and the title was turned over to Woburn High School.

While understandably disappointed, the honesty of Rota and his team did not go unnoticed. In November of that same year they were awarded a sportsmanship trophy by the state Attorney General, who had recently organized a group of New England's professional sports teams and officials desiring to promote better sportsmanship.

This story takes on a personal note also. This author graduated from Westborough High School in 1965. During that time I competed with the high school golf team that won the state championship in two consecutive years, 1964 and 1965. I find it most admirable that Greg Rota and his student-athletes are preserving the true spirit of the game and projecting the image for which the game has become known.

As a climax to this section on honesty, we present a situation that not only demonstrates the virtue of honesty, but also strengthens the argument for encouraging children to play golf.

There are many reasons why a parent would want to encourage a child to become involved in golf. Because of its physical requirements, it's a great way to improve natural endurance and agility. Monetarily, there's always the chance that the child might develop into an accomplished player and ultimately play the game for a living. However, the definitive reason is that the game has the potential to inspire the character traits of honesty and integrity. Such is the case of Douglas, Florida High School student Kyle Hitchcock.

During the 2001 regional golf championships, Hitchcock, who was a sophomore at the time, shot a fine 75. His tribulation came when he saw that his score was posted on the board as a 74. When he realized what had happened—his fellow competitor marking his card had given him a four on the ninth hole instead of a five—he faced a crossroads in his young life. It was one of those moments that would define his character.

He knew that his marker had no idea that an error had been made. He was also well aware of the rules of golf and the integrity of the game. Rule 6.6(D) requires disqualification of a player who signs for a score on a hole lower than actually taken. There is no rule for breach of integrity except in the conscience of the individual.

The path that he decided to choose would affect more than him. His actions would have far-reaching effects. If he said nothing and allowed the 74 to stand, he would be the medalist in the tournament—a great accomplishment for a sophomore. With his 74 he and his team would qualify for the following week's state championship. With his disqualification, neither he nor his team would enjoy that privilege. Then there was the consideration of family. His honesty would ruin his brother's last opportunity to play in the state championship. His brother was a senior. Finally, there was peer pressure. Surely embarrassment would be a consequence of his actions.

But Hitchcock knew exactly what must be done. He sought out his coach, Jim Roper, and explained the circumstances to him. Roper immediately notified officials. After recovering from the shock and disappointment Hitchcock commented, "My first instinct was the officials made a mistake, but I asked to check my card and I saw the four and I knew. I was shocked and then I was mad at myself for not catching it. I felt badly for my team-mates, the seniors were all very supportive of me." But most importantly, he added, "I could have taken another path, but I knew I couldn't have dealt with my conscience. I can live with this decision."

In an age when the pressure to excel in sports at the high school level is at an overbearing level, Kyle's father, Gary Hitchcock, expressed his pride in his son, "Golf creates clean-cut, outstanding young men. It's like the Ma-rines. Golf really is character building. It creates gentlemen."

A LITTLE KNOWLEDGE...

No matter where life takes us, knowledge is an essential element to make the journey successful. This is especially true concerning the career that one chooses to pursue. It goes without saying that knowledge is essential to be successful. Knowing the rules and traditions of one's profession is the key to job security and financial stability. The world of professional golf is no exception. Yet, despite the opportunity for advanced education on the rules of golf (there are USGA schools, PGA schools, seminars, videos and CDs) and the constant presence of rules officials, players on the professional tours of the world continue to display an amazing lack of knowledge regarding the rules.

Whenever you see a rules official being called to assist a player in a professional tournament, it is usually not the result of an awkward, out-of-the-ordinary rules situation. Rather, it is usually the insecurity of the player as to how to proceed under the rules. That's obvious when you observe the number of situations cited in this book. You may find yourself asking, "How could he do that?" or "How could he not know that?" There are also statistical facts. In a 2001 testing of selected professionals on the PGA Tour by *Golf Magazine*, the pros scored a paltry 54.4 percent. The test was brief yet fairly comprehensive with only one "stumper" question.

The timeworn adage "ignorance is bliss" is not applicable to the rules of golf, especially if one is trying to make his living playing the game. Ignorance is usually penalized by one or two strokes or worse—disqualification. Just examine the following cases.

———

One of the better publicized occurrences in the not-so-distant past transpired during the 1987 San Diego Open. While in contention during the third round, Craig

Stadler's errant tee shot on the par-4 14th settled under a pine tree. Stadler had two options: declare an unplayable lie or play the ball from the spot where it lay. He chose the latter. However, because of the pine tree, Stadler was forced to hit the shot from his knees. Being the astute dresser that he is, he placed a towel on the ground to protect his pants. No problem. He hit the shot and his knees stayed clean. When he finished, he signed his card. The next day on a "delayed" instant replay, he made the highlights. AT&T and Ma Bell did a great business. "He can't do that!" All during the fourth round Craig was chasing the leaders. He finished second—he thought. Rule 13.3 states that a player cannot build a stance. The penalty for a violation of the rule is two strokes, which were not accounted for on his scorecard. Thus he incurred the penalty of disqualification for signing an incorrect scorecard.

Some years later the offending tree became diseased (probably the result of a Stadler curse) and needed to be removed. Guess who was given the privilege of delivering the first blow with an axe?

———————

All golfers have experienced the agony of having a putt hang right on the lip. So did Andy Bean in the third round of the 1983 Canadian Open. Since the 10-second time limit was not yet in effect, we can assume Mr. Bean waited not more than a few seconds, then tapped it in—albeit with the grip of his putter. The penalty according to Rule 14.1—the ball must be struck with head of the club—is two strokes. The next day he missed a playoff by two strokes. To Mr. Bean's credit, he frankly admitted his lack of attention to detail: "All right," he said, "it was a dumbass thing to do."

———————

Everyone hates to play in a cold rain. Most won't even attempt it unless it's absolutely necessary. LPGA players Alexandra Reinhardt and Susan Grams were no exception. Playing together in a cold downpour during the final round of the 1983 Chrysler Plymouth Classic, the pair employed the use of hand warmers. Obviously good common sense. But, in the process of keeping their hands warm, Ms. Reinhardt and Ms. Grams also managed to keep their golf balls tepid. The problem is that hand warmers are to be used strictly for the hands, not the golf balls. Rule 5 (The Ball) and its resulting decisions provide guidance for this situation. Basically the rule says that the player cannot "influence" the ball. The penalty for a breach of Rule 5 is disqualification, which was assessed to both players.

———————

We all know that you are not allowed to improve your lie and it should be safe to assume that all professional golfers are aware of this. "Play the ball as you find it" is one of the two basic principles of the rules of golf (the other is "Play the course as you find it"). Rule 13 elaborates what a player may or may not do with concern to improving his lie, the area of his intended stance or swing or his line of play.

Ron Streck was certainly sensitive to this basic principle of the game. He was a veteran of the PGA Tour and a tournament winner. Playing in the 1982 Tournament of Champions, Streck was penalized for improving his lie. The problem was that he didn't know he'd done it. All he did was move a few branches that happened to be on the line of his intended swing. Regrettably, this action was in front of millions of television viewers and the 1-800-RE-

PORT-A-RULE switchboards at the network lit up. Fortunately for Streck all this happened before he signed his scorecard and he only had to endure the two-stroke penalty.

The life and legend of John Daly now rivals that of Paul Bunyan. He drives the golf ball farther than any mortal ever has. He can overcome great obstacles to accomplish his task. But, despite his Bunyanesque stature, he is still not immune to an occasional run-in with the rules.

During the 1996 Volvo Scandinavian Masters, Daly had an encounter with the rules that illustrates how detailed and subtle they can be. Daly was assessed a two-stroke penalty for unintentionally improving his lie. His crime? While preparing to hit a shot from the fairway, Daly brushed away sand from in front of his ball. This is a violation of Rule 13.2, which states that you cannot improve your line of play by removing sand. You can remove loose impediments, including stones, leaves, twigs, branches and the like.

All this is in force until you reach the green. Once on the green, sand is considered a loose impediment. Is this a bit perplexing? The reasoning goes like this: Sand and loose soils are considered to be natural parts of the golf course. But if sand is on the putting green, it is considered out-of-place. So if you are on the putting green you may remove sand and loose soil with your club or hand.

———

While I have placed the following incident under the heading of Knowledge, it also illustrates how forthright touring professionals are. Regardless of the rules quandary in which they may find themselves, they always seek to act with a sense of fairness. In this situation, however, it was the player's lack of knowledge on an extremely complex point in the rules that led to his mistake. This further demonstrates just how complicated the process of lifting, dropping and placing the ball can become. At the time of this incident, Rule 20.2 (B) declared that a ball was to be dropped "as near as possible to the spot where the ball lay, but not nearer the hole." Contrast that with how the rule reads now, "not nearer the hole than the specific spot which, if it is not precisely known, shall be estimated." Does this all seem to be bathed in minutiae and lathered in confusion? Well, it was to Bernhard Langer during the final round of the 1987 European Open at Walton Heath. *The Guardian* of September 14, 1987 reported it this way:

Langer, the overnight leader, had started with three straight pars when he drove into the rough at the fourth. He had a swing, but not much of one, and in attempting to hit the ball too far, struck it into the tree, never to be seen again.

Now, of course, he had to retreat to the spot from which he had played his second shot and drop another ball, which he did. But the ball jumped forward, ahead of the divot mark that Langer had located as being the spot from which he had previously played. The West German, seeking to be fair and thinking that he could not play his ball from a spot that was clearly nearer the hole, picked it up and redropped.

But Mike Stewart, a PGA official who was watching, was aghast. He raced over in his buggy, told Langer that not only was he in error and the ball he picked up was in play, he would also incur yet another penalty shot if he played the ball from where it now lay.

Langer had to replace the ball in the position it had occupied after the original drop and play out the hole. With the penalty for the lost ball and the penalty for picking up a ball in play, it cost him a triple-bogey seven and, effectively, his chances of winning.

This whole incident raises a couple of questions: Why did Mike Stewart not become involved in the situation earlier, which may have prevented Langer from having to incur any penalty shots? Why did Langer not call for a rules official if he had the slightest doubt as to the procedure? Questions, of course, to which we may never determine the answer.

It's a rare occurrence when a touring professional runs out of golf balls and for Champions Tour player John Jacobs it proved to be costly. One week after winning the 2003 Senior PGA Championship, Jacobs ran out of Stratas on the 54th and final hole of the Farmers Charity Classic. He then accepted a Titleist from a spectator and finished the hole. However, it wasn't until after he had signed his scorecard and failed to include a two-stroke penalty that he remembered the one ball rule that the PGA has in effect. Jacobs called the tournament office and informed them of the violation. Ultimately he was disqualified for signing an incorrect scorecard.

———————

Sometimes a player may have total knowledge of a point in the rules, but for some unknown reason, develops a case of temporary amnesia, and, although unintentionally, still breaks the rule.

Veteran Harrison Frazier experienced such a moment during the early rounds of the 2003 HP Classic in New Orleans. During a delay in play Frazier was having the usual golf-related chat with one of his playing partners. The conversation turned to the subject of training aids, always guaranteed to produce lively banter. As luck would have it, Frazier happened to have his favorite golf gizmo in his bag. In fact he was so proud of it that he proceeded to give a short demonstration. Whoops! That's a violation of Rule 7 (Practice). When Harrison came to his senses, he notified a rules official and it was determined that he had broken the rules. A two-stroke penalty was assessed.

———————

The guidelines defining the procedures for a provisional ball are not especially tricky. In fact the definition of a provisional ball gives us the rule (27.2) and the circumstances under which a provisional ball may be played. It's really pretty straightforward: You may play a provisional ball if you believe that your ball is out-of-bounds or lost OUTSIDE of a water hazard. Other than those circumstances, it is not permitted or necessary. It's a basic rule that even a semi-experienced golfer understands.

So what would prompt a world-class superstar to violate this rule? It's either a total lack of knowledge or a temporary case of golf rule amnesia. In Greg Norman's case during the 2004 Honda Classic it was the latter and the whole set of circumstances proved to be a comedy of errors. Norman was even par and in good shape to make the cut when he came to the 13th hole in the second round. The hole is a par-4 with a dogleg right that features a water hazard along the right side. It was in this direction that Norman sent his tee shot. After playing partners Fred Couples and Charles Howell III hit their tee shots, Norman announced that he was hitting a provisional ball. Error number one. A provisional ball is neither required nor legal if a player believes the ball to be in a water hazard. The ball was certainly not lost despite the fact that the marshals did not clearly indicate whether the ball was in the hazard or not.

Once Norman played his so-called provisional ball, it became the ball in play. He was really exercising one of his options for a ball that had come to rest in a water hazard. But Norman marched up to his original tee shot, which had come to rest in a bunker, and then proceeded to play his shot from there. Error number two. Even on-course television commentator Roger Maltbie tried to explain his error to him, but Norman replied, "Fine, then give me two shots. I'm not the rules guy here."

A PGA Tour rules official explained the situation to Norman, who refused to go back to the fairway and play the correct ball. At that point Norman would have been laying five in the fairway playing his sixth shot (he would have been assessed a two-stroke penalty for playing a wrong ball). Norman's simple statement settled the matter, "I'm disqualified." Then he left.

———————

These final two situations could be subtitled "A Little Knowledge is a Dangerous Thing" or "The Inevitable." They happened to a pair of PGA Tour Pros who have played a key role in the production of rules communication. One shows a player's unawareness of the rules, while the other demonstrates how detailed knowledge of the rules can work to one's advantage.

In the 1970s Johnny Miller was a PGA Tour superstar before becoming a color analyst for televised golf. Throughout his career, Miller won the 1973 U.S. Open and the 1976 British Open in addition to 23 PGA Tour events. In 1997 Miller hosted a USGA-produced CD entitled *The Rules of Golf*. This is only worth noting when you consider that Miller was involved in a rule mistake resulting from an apparent lack of knowledge of the rules.

During the Masters approximately 25 years ago, Miller's ball stopped on the side of a small but steep slope adjacent to the green. The slope was tilting toward the green. As touring pros are apt to do, Miller walked toward the green to get a look at his shot. But as Miller was heading back, his ball began to roll down the slope and finally came to rest on the green. Wow, what luck! But Miller did not accept his good fortune. Figuring this was against the understood "fairness" principle, Miller picked up the ball and put it back on the hill. Big mistake and a one-stroke penalty. Since the ball "had a mind of its own" and was not influenced by any action that Miller had taken (see Rule 18), he was entitled to leave his ball on the green.

In conclusion, here's a good example of why it helps to know the rules and all your options, especially in relief situations. In the 1996 PGA Championship played at Valhalla Golf Club in Louisville, Kentucky, Tom Watson dumped his ball into a water hazard on number 13 during the final round. Watson then took his relief about 30 yards behind the hazard. Why not just a couple of club-lengths in back of the hazard you ask? Well, the rules allow for either or anywhere in between. Rule 26.1(B) permits a player to drop a ball as near or as far back as desired. All you have to do is keep a straight line from the flagstick and the point where the ball last crossed the margin of the hazard. By dropping the ball some 30 yards behind the hazard, Watson was able to take a fuller swing and put more spin on the ball giving him more control over the shot.

So, how did Watson get so smart? You may remember Watson helped to author an excellent illustrative book on the rules of golf along with Frank Hannigan. He obviously paid attention to what he was doing.

ADVICE

Rule 8 (Advice Indicating Line of Play) and Rule 9 (Information as to Strokes Taken) are the only two rules under which a player can be penalized due to something he has said. Violations of Rule 8 are infrequent and usually not intentional. In most cases where there is a violation, the infraction arises from the player not totally understanding the rule. Rule 9 is seldom encountered in Professional Tournament play. It is almost exclusively applicable to match play. However, in stroke play one is allowed to inquire of his fellow competitor how many strokes he has taken. More communication of this sort could possibly eliminate several of the annual scoring mistakes where a player signs for a score either higher or lower than he has actually taken.

The rule pertaining to giving and requesting advice is unambiguous: Aside from one's caddy, partner or partner's caddy, a player cannot give or request advice. Advice is "any counsel or suggestion which could influence a player in determining his play, the choice of a club or the method of making a *stroke*." Except for tournament competition, everyone's Saturday morning foursome is a perpetual violator of the rule. "What'd you hit there, Bill?" is perhaps the most common phrase heard on the golf course. In the pro ranks there is a way around this. While one player is hitting, another player or his caddy "peeks" into the other's bag to see what club he's using. It's legal, but not ethical, and it's an all too frequent occurrence. A lot of players don't like this tactic. They feel it's against the spirit of the rule. Sometimes even the slightest slip of the tongue, whether it is in jest or in anger, can lead to a violation of this rule. Such a burst of anger can also be expensive.

Australian Greg Chalmers learned a $95,000 lesson concerning this rule in the 2001 Kemper Insurance Open at the TPC of Avenel in Potomac, Maryland. During the first round after a poor tee shot on a par-3, Chalmers noticed a  caddy peeking into his bag to see what he had hit. In the heat of the moment he fired off some verbiage to the offending caddy proclaiming his club of choice and the distance the caddy should keep away from his bag.

By the letter of the rule that's a violation and should result in a two-stroke penalty. However, no one in the group thought anything of the exchange, including Chalmers. It wasn't until Sunday night when he heard of a similar incident on the Buy.com Tour that Chalmers realized he had violated Rule 8, intentionally or not.

Chalmers informed tournament director Mark Russell, who had no choice but to apply the penalty. Of course, that started a chain reaction. Since the penalty had not been applied at the time of the infraction or at least before the scorecard was signed, Chalmers was guilty of signing an incorrect scorecard and was disqualified. The tragic part of this whole situation is that he was tied for 12th place at nine under par with one hole to play in the rain-delayed tournament. If he had parred the last hole, Chalmers would have won nearly $95,000.

To further aggravate the situation, if bad weather had not caused the Kemper to extend into Monday and the tournament had been completed on Sunday as usual, Chalmers would have been able to keep his check because it would have been too late to penalize him. The tournament would have been fully completed.

———————————————

For another testimony that violation of this rule can be expensive and create hard feelings, consider the following incident that occurred during the 1998 Southern PGA Club Professional Championship. It demonstrates how detailed and hairsplitting this rule really is and how the fun of competition can be expunged regardless of the level of competition.

During the first round of the tournament, a rules official was approached on the 16th hole and asked to mediate a rules situation that had occurred on the previous hole. One player in the group had hit his ball into the pine trees. After locating his ball the player yelled at another player in his group asking what his yardage to the green was. The queried player responded by informing him that he was not allowed to provide him with that information.

From there the situation went downhill. The player whose ball was in the trees interpreted the response as unsportsmanlike. As a result tension had begun to build up in the group and the situation needed to be resolved.

Here's how it was handled. After completion of the 17th hole, the rules official approached the player and asked if he had indeed asked another player what his yardage was. He confessed that he had, but felt that he was within the rules according to Rule 8. Close, but…According to Decision 8-1/2, it is permissible to request yardage from a permanent object, but not from a non-permanent object such as your ball. Thus, he was in violation of Rule 8.1 and was assessed a two-stroke penalty.

There is also a good bit of education here. The player who had been asked for the advice did indeed respond in the proper manner by stating that he could not provide that information. Had he given the yardage to the other player, he too would have been guilty of violating Rule 8.1 and would also have been assessed a two-stroke penalty.

But, wait—there's more. Before the rules official could make his final decision, he needed to determine that the player had not requested the yardage in order to determine who was away. Decision 8-1/2.5 permits the exchange of distance information in order to determine the order of play.

THE CADDY

The world of professional golf may look like a solo operation, but in reality it's a two-man team. It's the player and the caddy. While the caddy is virtually extinct at the local club level today, on the professional tours throughout the world the caddy is a vital part of the player's success. There is a bond of trust that must be established and maintained between the player and the caddy. If for any reason that trust is broken, then the caddy is usually dismissed.

On the surface it looks like a pretty fundamental job—carry the clubs, clean the clubs, get the yardage and replace the divots. These are the visible, physical tasks, the ones that are seen on television week after week. But behind the scenes there's a lot more to the job. The caddy must be an amateur psychologist, constantly providing encouragement and infusing his player with injections of confidence. At times the caddy must be a meteorologist providing atmospheric pressure, wind speed and temperature, all to be considered with yardage and elevation and a few other nebulous factors, then hand his player the proper club and pray that he has figured the equation correctly. Among the less discernible responsibilities is a working knowledge of the rules. The rulebook considers the player and the caddy as one. Whatever action a caddy takes has the potential of affecting his player. Rule 6.4 states, "For any breach of a Rule by his caddy, the player incurs the applicable penalty." Therefore, it is essential that the caddy knows at all times what he can and cannot do within the confines of the rules.

Experienced caddies generally do have a good knowledge of the rules. Inexperienced ones, to include friends of the player, are most likely to be limited in their familiarity with the rules despite their enthusiasm for the job. Rules official Ralph Bernhisel had the following situation during the 1997 PGA Championship at Winged Foot (the names have been kept anonymous in the annals of history).

An unnamed player had a pitch shot over a bunker on the 12th hole. However, he hit the shot fat and the ball and the divot came to rest in the bunker. In his enthusiasm, the caddy, who was a friend of the player and working for the thrill of being involved in a major championship, immediately ran forward and grabbed the divot from the bunker. That's a no-no.

A divot is considered a loose impediment. Rule 13.4(C) prohibits the removal of a loose impediment from a hazard if one's ball is in the hazard. Because of the actions of his caddy, the player was assessed a two-stroke penalty for a violation of the rule just as if he had removed the divot himself.

One would assume that a touring professional would make an excellent and experienced caddy. Not necessarily. Fred Couples, being the good guy that he is and having nothing to do on the Monday before the 1988 K-Mart Greater Greensboro Open, decided to caddy for his longtime pal Tom Petri in the qualifier. Wow! What more could you ask for? How about a two-stroke penalty? On the ninth hole Petri pulled his drive to the left into some deep grass. Couples performed his duty as a caddy most honorably. He found the ball—at least he thought he did. Petri played the ball that Couples found and they headed toward the green. Ten steps later they found another ball. Bad luck. It was Petri's real ball. Couples had identified the wrong ball and Petri didn't bother to check. That's a two-stroke penalty and now he had to play the original ball.

———————————

The care, keeping and counting of the clubs are some of the unpretentious but vital tasks of the caddy. Rule 4.4(A) states that a player can have not more than 14 clubs in the bag during a round of golf. Any more than that and there's a penalty—Match Play: minimum—one hole, maximum—two holes; Stroke Play: minimum—two strokes, maximum—four strokes. For golf history enthusiasts the rule limiting the number of clubs to 14 was instituted in 1938 by the USGA. The R&A had rejected such a proposal a year earlier, but in 1939 acquiesced and adopted the rule. Prior to this time there was no limit on the number of clubs a player could have available to him.

Perhaps the most stinging and publicized gaffe by a caddy in recent tournament play occurred in the 2001 British Open at Royal Lytham & St. Anne's. Ian Woosnam, experiencing a resurrection of his career, began the final round just one stroke out of the lead held by Niclas Fasth of Sweden. Woosnam's tee shot on the opening hole, a medium iron par-3, stopped just six inches from the hole. The tap-in birdie should have put him in a tie for the lead. However, when he got to the second tee his caddy, Miles Byrne, informed him that something was terribly wrong. There was an extra club in the bag, a second driver that Woosnam had been practicing with on the range. Woosnam, frustrated and angry, took the extra club out of the bag and tossed it across the tee in disgust. The extra club and the two-stroke penalty that goes along with it turned the first hole birdie into a bogey. The situation naturally upset Woosnam, who followed with a couple of more bogeys before regaining his composure. There is, of

course, no way to tell precisely just how much the penalty cost Woosnam, but a bit of arithmetic reveals that it meant a six-way tie for third instead of solo second, a difference of $312,326 and Ryder Cup points—not to mention a chance at his second major championship.

To Woosnam's credit he did not dismiss Byrne on the spot or immediately after the round. "He's a good caddy," Woosnam proclaimed. "He won't do it again." Byrne and Woosnam had joined together in the spring after Woosnam had encouraged his longtime caddy Phillip Morbey to find another bag that might be more financially beneficial. But alas, Woosnam's patience wore out later in the season when Byrne failed to be punctual and he dismissed him.

One might wonder how the mistake of carrying more than 14 clubs could ever occur—especially on the professional tours. But the Woosnam incident is not the sole occurrence. Also during the 2001 season, Ignacio Garrido and his caddy could not get the math correct and wound up with more than 14 clubs during the English Open.

Evidently Garrido's math skills are somewhat limited. The same situation befell him three years earlier during the 1998 British Masters. Garrido was assessed a four-stroke penalty. That's the maximum for exceeding the 14-club limit on more than one hole according to Rule 4.4. After 72 holes he finished tied for fourth, two strokes behind the winner.

Furthermore, to add a little humor to all of this but not at the expense of just how serious the Rules can be, consider the misfortune of Glenn Ralph's female caddy. During one tournament round in the 2001 European Tour season, she "discovered" a child's putter in the bag. She tried to reason her way out of the mess by exclaiming: "It's only a small putter, does it matter?"

"Yes, it matters," growled the tournament rules officials. It also mattered in a big way to Ralph. The error cost Ralph his place in that tournament and his player's card at the end of the year.

Strangely enough, this has happened before. LPGA player Dale Eggeling had the same situation in the 1992 JC Penney Classic. Now bear in mind, this is a team event pairing a PGA pro and an LPGA pro. Usually the format is a modified alternate shot so any penalty gets added to the team score. In the middle of the back nine Eggeling hit her approach to the green and gave the iron back to her caddy. But the club wouldn't fit in the bag. So the caddy investigated the problem. What do you think he found at the bottom of the bag? An itty-bitty 7-iron, the property of Dustin Eggeling, Dale's four- year-old son. But the size of the club is no concern to the rulebook. It's a two-stroke penalty for each hole that an extra club is in the bag with a maximum of four strokes. The team's score for Eggeling and her partner Wayne Levi went from 74 to 78.

Now consider this riddle. When is an extra club not considered a club even though it's a club? Answer: When it's your child's plastic club. Just ask Nancy Lopez, who also found an extra club in her bag during the 1992 season. Fortunately, it was one of her children's plastic clubs and since it does not fit the rulebook definition of a club, Lopez was not penalized.

———

Not only is the counting of the clubs important, but the safekeeping of the clubs is also a critical task for the caddy.

Just imagine the chagrin of Jose Manuel Carriles's caddy when he was unable to locate the 7-iron of his boss on the 14th hole of a recent event on the European Tour. It seems he had left it on the 12th green. On the 14th Carriles needed that club again. The caddy was sent to retrieve the lost club and that he did. But the time lost was critical and when he returned with the club Carriles had already been assessed a two-stroke penalty for slow play. After 36 holes Carriles missed the cut by one stroke.

———

In the 1978 Quad Cities Open, Leonard Thompson's caddy was attempting to coax the ball into the hole with a bit of body language when a tee that had been stuck behind his ear fell onto the ball, deflecting it from the hole. As if that was not bad enough, Thompson was then penalized two strokes for striking his own equipment.

———

When the U.S. Open resumed in 1946 after an interruption from 1942-45 due to World War II, the venue was the Canterbury Golf Club in Cleveland, Ohio. A rare rules inci-

dent involving a caddy occurred during regulation play that had a direct effect on the outcome of the tournament. On the final day during the third round (at that time the U.S. Open ended on Saturday with 36 holes of play), Byron Nelson was near the top of the leaderboard. In 1946, crowd control was not as critical or precise as it is today. Spectators were allowed to run rampant over the course, virtually unchecked by gallery ropes. The only crowd control that existed was a few ropes that the marshals dragged around and pulled tight in an effort to restrain the crowd. It was not until 1954 that crowd control (basically roping off the tees, fairways and greens) was introduced at the U.S. Open. This lack of crowd control and spectator discipline eventually cost Nelson. After he played his second shot on the par-5 13th, the crowd surged ahead. In his attempt to get to his player's ball, Nelson's caddy pushed through the unruly crowd, lost his balance and accidentally stepped on Nelson's ball. The penalty: one stroke. Tragically, this one-stroke penalty put Nelson into a three-way playoff with Lloyd Mangrum and Vic Ghezzi at the end of regulation play. The playoff was won by Mangrum over 36 holes the next day. It is no small wonder that this was Nelson's last U.S. Open. Burned out from the rigors and pressure of competitive golf, Nelson retired at the age of 34.

Hand-to-eye coordination skills should also be on the resume of the caddy. Being able to catch a toss of the ball by the player can be a most essential skill. At the 2001 English Open, an incident occurred between Raymond Russell and his caddy, Clark Ingram. On the 71st green Russell tossed Ingram the ball to clean, but Ingram missed the toss. The ball disappeared into the lake that fronts the green. Into the lake waded Ingram in an attempt to find the ball. His fishing and fumbling proved unsuccessful and

Russell was penalized two strokes for not finishing the hole with the ball with which he started. The miscue cost Russell about 4,000£ when he went from 10th to 16th place. Nevertheless, the Scottish Russell displayed a typical sense of humor: "Let's say he is a Scottish goalkeeper."

You think this is a rare occurrence? The same thing happened to Mark Brooks in the 1991 Las Vegas Invitational. In the fourth round of the event Brooks marked his ball on the 18th green and tossed it to his caddy. Whoops! He missed it and the ball trickled down the slope and into the lake beside the green. This time Brooks went after the ball (it's not on record why the caddy did not head into the abyss), but to no avail. Add two strokes and give Mr. Brooks a double-bogey on the hole.

The job becomes even trickier when more than one skill is involved. What if a player is having a tough hole and his score is going higher and higher? It's then that the caddy earns his keep. At that critical juncture of the round, the caddy walks the fine line between encourager and counselor. Should he attempt to inspire confidence, should he console or should he just keep his mouth shut? Most players would probably prefer the latter.

But what if the caddy is suddenly inflicted with a muscular spasmodic attack? What if all muscle memory is suddenly erased from the computer in the brain? For such an occurrence he is doomed and subject to the emotional fancy of his player.

As an example of the above scenario we present Tsuneyuki (Tommy) Nakajima and his caddy in the 1978 Masters. When Mr. Nakajima and his bag-toting assistant reached the par-5 13th they were in good stead with par, but unaware that they were about to make history. After an acceptable drive around the corner on the 465-yard dogleg left, Nakajima decided to go for the green. But alas, disaster! His approach came up short and found the creek that snakes its way around the green. Facing a dilemma to play it or take a penalty shot, Nakajima quickly determined that the ball was playable and gave it a whack. Nothing, so he figured he had the wrong club and decided to change. About this time the juggling act became too much for his caddy. As the caddy attempted to juggle a towel, two clubs and a golf bag while maintaining his balance on the bank of the creek, he dropped the newly requested club and it hit the ball. Whoops! That's a two-stroke penalty for moving a ball in a hazard. Eventually the nightmare ended with double digits on the scorecard, a 13 to be exact, and nary a word from his caddy. Sadly, the historians have failed us; the eventual fate of the caddy is unknown.

TIME

The issue of time in the game of golf is seldom considered as an influence in the outcome of an event. Golf is a sport that is generally not confined by the boundaries of space and time in a way that most other sports are. There are no standard dimensions for the playing arena (there is only one—the hole is 4.25-inches in diameter) and the duration of the game is not restricted by a definitive time boundary, even though the subjective term "undue delay" is mentioned in the rulebook. Yet, the concept of time appears more frequently in the rulebook than one might readily imagine. And there are instances where the issue of time has been pivotal during a round of golf.

Two incidents of recent vintage undoubtedly determined the outcome of major championships: the 1998 U.S. Open and the 1998 British Open.

Rule 6 explains a player's responsibilities. Within those six pages Rule 6.3(A) is time oriented in that it establishes the criteria and penalty for the Time of Starting. The recommended penalty is disqualification, however, the committee may institute a qualification that permits a player to arrive within five minutes of his tee time and be assessed a two-stroke penalty in stroke play or loss of the first hole in match play. Rule 6.7 informs the player that he must proceed in the playing of the game without undue delay. He is not permitted to fiddle around between holes and delay play and he must maintain the pace of play guidelines that the committee has established. Note 2 under this section gives the committee permission to establish time constraints for the competitors to complete a stipulated round, hole or stroke. It should be noted that virtually all professional tours have procedures in place to deter slow play. Whether these procedures are enforced is another matter. It is also another matter whether these procedures are administered uniformly or arbitrarily. The most celebrated case was the disqualification of Seve Ballesteros in the 1980 U.S. Open.

There are two time-specific rules that may affect the actual playing of the game. One is the maximum time permitted for a player to search for a lost ball. The other involves the maximum time permitted for a player to wait for a ball to fall that is overhanging the hole. Interestingly, one is through the green; the other is on the green. "Through the green" is a term used to describe the area of the golf course except tees, greens and hazards. The manner in which a player may proceed on the green as opposed to through the green may at times be different. Ultimately, it is the player's responsibility to know the correct procedures. Each year on the professional tours of the world there are, unfailingly, several incidents involving each rule.

In the "Definitions" section of the rulebook the wording is specific concerning the amount of time that a player is allowed to look for his ball—five minutes once he has reached the point where he believes the ball to be and begins to look for the ball (this rule first appeared in 1783 in a rules code developed by golfers in Aberdeen, Scotland). A ball is lost if it has not been found or identified by the player during the allotted five minutes. If the ball is lost, the player continues in accordance with the procedure under Rule 27.1. This rule seems simple enough on the surface. You are permitted five minutes to look. If you don't find your ball, then it's lost. However, the actual interpretation and application of this rule can become complex.

The following two cases are directly related in that the first was used to interpret the second about a month later. They demonstrate how five minutes can be five minutes plus. The year was 1998 and the United States golf community was engaged in Tiger mania, as was a great part of the rest of the world. But the attention of the fans in the major championships had fallen on Lee Janzen in the U.S. Open and Mark O'Meara in the Masters and the British Open. The claim by the USGA and the R&A that the rules are there to help the player and not punish him was never more evident as O'Meara and Janzen went on to victory. Both Janzen in the U.S. Open and O'Meara in the British Open marched to victory with the help of the "find it in five minutes" rule.

The 1998 U.S. Open was at the Olympic Club in San Francisco. If you're not familiar with Olympic, the course is tree-lined with tall cypress and pines that have a hunger for golf balls. At times they seem to swallow them and not spit them back.

Lee Janzen began the final day five shots behind leader Payne Stewart. By the time he reached the fifth tee, he trailed by six. Gambling with a wood off the tee, Janzen's tee ball sailed directly into one of the hungry cypress trees. The tree ate it up and didn't spit it out—at least not immediately. When Janzen and his caddy arrived at the area (and his five minutes began), an official confirmed that the ball had entered the tree, but not exited. The search party looked in the tree and saw nothing. They looked a bit longer and still nothing. Janzen, in accordance with Rule 27, headed back toward the tee. But wait! As he headed back, he heard his name. His caddy and a couple dozen other people were hollering that they had found his ball. A healthy gust of wind had loosened the tree's grip and the ball had fallen. Janzen returned, identified his ball and proceeded to make par on the hole. Even though he had given up the search before the allotted five minutes had expired, he had not put another ball into play and thus his ball was not "officially" lost. Janzen "found" his ball and avoided a potentially devastating two-stroke penalty. This break was the turning point of his round. From here Janzen played spectacular golf and went on to win the U.S. Open.

———————

Now fast-forward one month to the British Open at Royal Birkdale. It's the third round and Mark O'Meara and several others are chasing leader Brian Watts. They're all playing in what would be considered tropical storm winds. When he arrived on the sixth tee, O'Meara was already three over for the day and facing the toughest hole on the course—a 470-yard par-4 playing directly into a hurricane. O'Meara's drive was solid, but he still needed another driver off the fairway to reach the green. He pushed it right; it got caught in the wind and went further right, directly into the sand hills among some thick shrubbery. O'Meara and his caddy headed off to find the ball. The designated five minutes began when they reached the scene and the search commenced. They were also aided by an army of well-intentioned spectators who probably did not help the situation by trampling down the grass.

After four minutes nothing was found and O'Meara informed the official on the scene that his ball was a Strata with his personal logo on it. At this point O'Meara headed back to the point where he had hit his second shot. But with 30 seconds remaining, a cry of "We've got it" rang out. Both the official and O'Meara's caddy verified that the ball was indeed O'Meara's.

Frantically they called to O'Meara and got his attention before he hit another ball and that ball became the ball in play. As O'Meara headed back to the area of the found ball, a conference over the timing commenced involving a senior and more "expert" rules official. This new official ruled that since the player had not identified the ball within five minutes it was lost.

O'Meara was told to return again to the spot of his second shot.

But before O'Meara could head back to the spot of his original shot again, a final complication arose. R&A Officials, who had also come to the scene and who were in charge of administering the rules, overruled the official. Citing a principle accepted by the Joint USGA and R&A Committee, they declared that the ball was considered found within the five minutes despite the fact the player had not identified it. They affirmed, "It is permissible that the player's identification of the ball occur after the passage of the five minutes." R&A Officials were simply following the precedence established a month earlier in the Janzen case at the U.S. Open.

There is one further twist. During all the searching and confusion, a spectator had picked up the ball. Under the rules O'Meara was permitted to drop the ball as close as possible to the spot where it had been picked up. On both drops the ball rolled beyond the allotted two club-lengths limit and O'Meara was then permitted to place the ball on top of the already trampled grass, a huge advantage.

The bottom line interpretation: It is permissible that a ball can be found within the five-minute limit and identified by the player outside of the five-minute time limit.

Just as Janzen had done in the U.S. Open, O'Meara went on to win the British Open. O'Meara's victory came when he defeated Brian Watts in a playoff.

———

Rule 16.2 states that if a ball is overhanging the hole a player has 10 seconds once he reaches the hole to determine if the ball is at rest. If the ball does not fall into the hole during that 10-second time period, the ball is deemed to be at rest and must be promptly played. Any further delay results in a one-stroke penalty. It is this rule which occasionally causes great consternation despite the fact that this time limit has been in effect since 1984.

The inclusion of this 10-second limit was first instituted in 1984 in conjunction with the major reordering of the rules. The rule was the first inclusion into the rulebook of a specific time limit pertaining to a ball overhanging the hole. It imposed a penalty of loss of hole in match play and two-strokes in stroke play. In 1988 this severe penalty was reduced to its current status, a one-stroke penalty after the 10-second time limit has elapsed.

———————

In this age of escalating technology the players on the professional tours of the world are under increasing scrutiny by the watchful eye of the television camera and the viewing public. With its well-defined time restrictions, Rule 16.2 is easy to apply for the average golf fan. All he has to do is watch the television and count to 10. Lee Janzen is a case in point. Janzen received an unexpected 34th birthday present from several fans during the playing of the 1998 NEC World Series of Golf at the Firestone Country Club during the first round.

Janzen's seven-foot birdie putt on the 17th green seemed to hang on the lip of the cup forever. And it did. It hung for so long that several television spectators phoned in to the PGA Tour and snitched on Janzen—after the telecast had gone off the air at six p.m. and Janzen had already signed his card.

The scene on that green must have been comical. After Janzen putted and the ball halted one-16th of a turn from falling to the bottom of the cup, Janzen made his way to the hole without unreasonable delay in accordance with the rules. Now the comedy started. Janzen walked past the hole glancing at the ball, back to the hole and then bent down to observe the offending pellet. Finally, he summoned playing partner Vijay Singh to have a look. Singh came to the hole and also bent down to lend his observational opinion to the situation. At last, after a couple of shrugs of the shoulders, Janzen gripped his putter and went to tap the ball in. But, before he could get his putter on the ball, it fell in. Janzen, Singh and the crowd enjoyed a good laugh.

The problem was the amount of time that had elapsed while all the shenanigans around the hole were taking place. Replays by ESPN clocked Janzen at 27 seconds, though somehow PGA Tour officials "estimated" the time at 20 seconds.

Since Rule 16.2 set the time limit at 10 seconds and Janzen had more than doubled that, he should have recorded a four for the hole instead of the three that was put on the scorecard. Since he signed the card for a score lower than he actually had made, he was disqualified.

But Janzen did have a defense. He thought the ball was still moving, and, according to Rule 14.5, a "player shall not play while his ball is moving." PGA Tour rules official Mark Russell cleared up the matter, "After 10 seconds, the ball is considered at rest, whether it is or not." In other words, Rule 16.2 superseded Rule 14.5.

What's puzzling here is why Janzen did not consult with PGA Tour officials before signing his card. Surely he was aware of the rule. And why did not one of the hundreds of spectators mention the possibility of an infraction? Did no one know of the rule?

With the disqualification, Janzen received unofficial last place money of $18,475.

———

Brian Gay was also a victim of this rule during the 2000 Honda Classic. On the 17th green during the third round, Gay's putt stopped directly at the hole. Gay quickly moved to the hole but stopped short of tapping in the ball. Upon examining the situation, he too thought the ball was still moving and expressed such to his playing partner. Gay waited and waited, well past the 10-second limit. Finally the ball fell. But it was too late. Since the 10 seconds had elapsed, he was assessed a one-stroke penalty for violation of rule 16.2.

Curiously, the television replay showed that the ball may have been moving. But this rule does not take this into account. It is exact in its explanation. Once 10 seconds have expired the player can tap the ball into the hole with no fear of being assessed a penalty for hitting a moving ball. After 10 seconds the ball is deemed to be at rest.

———————

Promptness for one's tee time is vital. Rule 6.3 in the section on the Player's Responsibilities has a couple of explanatory paragraphs concerning starting times. It simply states that the player must show up punctually for his tee time or else he will be penalized. Rule 6.3(A) states, "The player shall start at the time laid down by the Committee." No sooner, no later. Usually this rule is enforced in connection with a player arriving late for his starting time. However, there is one outstanding case in which a player began his round earlier than the appointed time and suffered the consequences.

The final outcome of the 1940 U.S. Open will always be tarnished due to an unusual situation involving Ed "Porky" Oliver and his ultimate disqualification. The 72-hole championship proper ended in a tie at 287 between Gene Sarazen and Lawson Little. Oliver had also returned a score of 287 that would have tied him with Sarazen and Little, but he was one of six players who were disqualified for starting ahead of their official starting times.

In a hasty effort to beat an impending storm, all six had started their rounds in the absence of the official starter, Joe Dey of the USGA, who was in the clubhouse having lunch. To their credit and epitomizing the true sportsmanship of the game, Sarazen and Little determined between them to have Oliver included in the playoff. But the USGA stood firm; Oliver was disqualified.

Arriving at the tee box even just a few seconds late brings at the least a two-stroke penalty. Fortunately, it is a rare occurrence when we hear of a player being penalized for tardiness. Of course, if it does happen in a major championship, it resonates throughout the entire golf world. And if you happen to be one of the "young guns" of the golf world, the reverberation will be almost deafening.

Aaron Baddeley, 22-year-old Australian, a pretender to the superstar throne, is the youngest player to win the Australian Open at age 19. But in the 2003 PGA Championship, the youngster ran afoul of his personal time-keeping device. After shooting one under 69 in the first round, he was among the leaders of the championship just three strokes off the lead.

After making his preparations for the second round, Baddeley was standing around the clubhouse of the Oak Hill Golf Course at 7:29 a.m. just having a chat and waiting for what he thought was his 7:35 a.m. tee time. Just then he noticed his caddy, Fran Pirozzolo, making a beeline in his direction.

"You're on the clock," Pirozzolo breathlessly stated. "Try to look concerned. It might help."

Baddeley and Pirozzolo sprinted for the 10th tee but 150 yards later they were still 40 seconds late for the 7:30 a.m. tee time. The next conversation went something like this:

"You're late!" exclaimed the PGA rules official.

"Serious?" inquired Baddeley.

"As a heart attack," was the reply. "Two-stroke penalty."

So before he hit his first tee shot of the day, Baddeley instantly went from one under to one over. Baddeley drew little sympathy from PGA rules official Ralph Bernhisel, "Do we like it? It's our worst nightmare."

───────

Craig Stadler also learned the importance of punctuality in his Champions Tour debut. In the 2003 Senior PGA Championship at Aronimink just outside Philadelphia, the "Walrus" was only three strokes off the lead after 36 holes. Mysteriously, he showed up two minutes, 20 seconds late for his 10:05 a.m. Saturday starting time.

Stadler claimed that he had called the club on the previous evening and was informed that his Saturday tee time was 10:20. He arrived at the course with plenty of time to spare at 9:00 and was standing around the putting green when he was informed he was on the tee. It was too late. He was assessed a two-stroke penalty for being late for his tee time. Fortunately, he made it within the allotted five minutes and avoided disqualification. His chances for the championship wasted away with the time.

YOU CAN'T FOOL MOTHER NATURE

Since golf is an outdoor sport, players will constantly come in contact with Mother Nature. Of course, Mother Nature manifests herself in a great variety of forms on the golf course. The rulebook does not specifically mention nature or Mother Nature. But it does address several of her offspring. And often, by definition, a similar entity is separated. For instance, "casual water" includes the liquid variety of the substance as well as snow and natural ice. It does not include dew, frost and manufactured ice, however.

The realm of Mother Nature also includes the animal kingdom. The rulebook further separates the animal kingdom by definition: for example, burrowing animals and non-burrowing animals. "Burrowing animals" include the likes of rabbits, moles, ground hogs, gophers and salamanders. According to the USGA they are all similar because they make a hole for habitation or shelter. Conversely, an animal such as a dog or an alligator or a frog is not a burrowing animal. All this may seem a bit perplexing, which is why, if you're going to play golf outdoors, you may want to keep a rulebook handy. Whatever the definition, in all her various forms, even Mother Nature will occasionally exert her influence on the golf course.

————————————

Mother Nature does have a grand sense of humor and will from time to time take the opportunity to exhibit it on the golf course. During the 1978 Tournament Players Championship, J.C. Snead, nephew of the legendary Sam Snead and known for his prodigious straw hat, was over a putt when a gust of wind blew his hat onto his ball. Naturally, the ball moved. Rule 18.2(A)(2) states your equipment, except your clubhead, cannot cause the ball to move. Penalty: one stroke and the ball must be replaced.

———————————

Not only does Mother Nature have a sense of humor, but she is also non-discriminatory. She even picks on the great ones. On his way to victory in the 1961 British Open, Arnold Palmer endured a second round 73 that included a wind-aided seven at the 16th hole. Palmer's second shot had found a bunker, but, after he had taken his stance in preparation to play the shot, a strong gust of wind moved the ball. That's a one-stroke penalty despite the fact that it was a trick of Mother Nature.

———————————

In 1983 Nancy Maunder was a rookie on the LPGA Tour trying hard to make the cut, earn a check and stay alive. In an early season tournament, the

Arizona Copper Classic, she was all set to putt when a bee landed on her ball. Her caddy, being the chivalrous and exuberant sort, and certainly desiring the best advantage for his player, knelt and blew the bee

from the ball. The ball moved. Rule 18.2(A)(1) also states that your caddy cannot cause the ball to move. Penalty: one stroke and the ball must be replaced.

When you get to the Far East, Mother Nature has a different look, especially on the golf course. Nonetheless, the rules of golf still apply. In 1999 tournament officials on the Asian PGA Tour opened the season with a most curious rules situation. During the second round of the London Myanmar Open played in Yangon, Myanmar, local professional Too Aung found his opening tee shot lying gently against a fist-sized frog.

Aung was in disbelief, "I didn't know whether to hit the ball or not." Wisely, before playing "frog," he called for the rules officials. After considerable research, referees Dato

Murugesu and Doug Logan ruled that the frog was an outside agency. With tongue in cheek they encouraged him to tickle the frog to make it move. Fortunately it was a sensitive frog and immediately jumped. The ball moved but was replaced without penalty.

The tournament director was informed of the frog incident and astutely observed, "There is no specific rule to cover the ball coming to rest against a frog." But alas, poor Aung, the frog caper must have rattled his nerves. He bogeyed the hole and continued on posting a two-day total of 162, 18 over par, and the highest score in the 150-player field.

Appendix I in the rulebook grants the committee the privilege of establishing Local Rules for abnormal conditions. It states, "If local abnormal conditions interfere with the proper playing of the game…" Certainly in the interest of safety a crocodile pit would be included under this provision. Unfortunately Graeme Francis must not have been aware of this.

During the second round of the 2001 Dimension Data Pro-Am in South Africa, Graeme played his ball from a crocodile pit. The problem was that the committee had instituted the local rule that prohibited play from the pit. While pleading his case, Graeme defended his action by declaring there were no crocodiles present while he extricated his ball from the pit. The argument landed on deaf ears. He was disqualified.

———————

It seems right to place this incident under the chapter of Mother Nature, because the whole situation would never have occurred without Mother Nature's sweet little creatures. However, it quite logically could have been placed under Rules Officials or Relief. And it's too bad there is no rule on a golfer's attitude, for this would have fit there as well.

In attempting to qualify for the 2003 New Zealand Open, David Hartshorne became involved in a three-way playoff for the final spot in local qualifying. On the first hole of the playoff, Hartshorne faced a must-make

35-foot putt. Upon examining the line he discovered duck droppings and requested permission to remove them under the loose impediment rule. "No," said Tournament Director and Rules Official, Phil Aickin. "Those droppings have been stepped on, stuck to the green, baked by the sun and will not affect the roll of the ball." Hartshorne putted and missed, thus failing to move on to the next level of qualifying.

That should be the end of the story.

But wait, there's more! Usually the official's word is final, but this was not good enough for Hartshorne. He protested to the New Zealand PGA requesting that the decision be overturned and that he be permitted to play in the next level of qualifying. Hartshorne's protest prompted Aickin to further exhibit his knowledge on the rules of golf and duck poo in particular, "Fresh dung will sit there a couple of centimeters high, but once somebody stands on it, it flattens and it gets baked to the green and that was quite simply the situation," explained Aickin. "Besides, he had a one in 15 or 20 chance of making the putt anyway."

That seemed satisfactory for the PGA Tour chief executive Andrew Georgiou, who indicated that the matter would not reach the board and that he would stand with Aickin's decision. Hartshorne's appeal came to a dead end and that was, finally, the end of the matter.

———————

The following incident demonstrates precisely how complicated a ruling can become. It also points out how a player can be(e) "stung" by a ruling.

The 1997 PGA Championship was held on the West Course at Winged Foot Country Club in Mamaroneck, New York. This A.W. Tillinghast design was anticipated to be "rule friendly" for the tournament. However, during the second round Rules Official Mark Wilson was called to the par-3 10th hole to render an interwoven ruling involving Mother Nature.

Rick Fehr's tee shot had almost buried halfway up one of the steep faced bunkers and was barely visible. This in itself would present no problem. The ball must be played as it lies. What did present a problem was a bee hole in close proximity that was causing the sand to shift and cover the ball. From here the ruling became more complicated as Wilson analyzed the situation. Rule 25.1 permits relief from a hole, cast or runway made by a burrowing animal, a reptile or a bird. When the ball lies in or touches such a condition or the condition interferes with the player's stance or area of intended swing, the player is entitled to relief. Simply drop the ball in the bunker, not nearer the hole and as close as possible to the original spot, but away from the abnormal ground condition. This is true if the ball lies in a bunker, but is not applicable in a water hazard or lateral water hazard. Such a condition in a water hazard is considered normal since water hazards are viewed as the normal habitat of burrowing animals, reptiles or birds (in such a case proceed under Rule 26.1).

If the rules become this detailed and involved, why not go further in an attempt to get Fehr relief? Two questions arise: First, is a bee a burrowing animal? Wilson ruled no. If a bee is an insect, then an insect is only a loose impediment as defined by *The Rules of Golf*. Therefore, Fehr did not receive relief and had to play the ball as it lie without removing the impediment.

But what if these "bees" in question were hornets? Hornets make their nests (habitat) in the ground. If this species of bee were identified as a hornet, would it then be considered a burrowing animal? Unfortunately for Fehr, the rules are not detailed enough as yet to distinguish the type of bee or insect.

Second, was there a "dangerous situation" involved? Wilson again said "No." He based his decision partly on the fact that he (Wilson) observed only a "couple" of bees and Fehr was therefore not entitled to relief because of a "dangerous situation" (see Decisions 1-4/10 and 1-4/11). But, by ruling that Fehr did not have a "dangerous situation," Wilson eliminated the possibility that Fehr could be allergic to bee stings. What if that was the case?

For the record, Fehr's first attempt to play the ball only dislodged it to the bottom of the bunker. His next try got it on the green.

And the habitat of Mother Nature's creatures remained undisturbed.

———

In golf there are birdies and then there are birds. Anytime you have water on a golf course you'll get certain species that have a natural inclination to the water. During the 1998 Players Championship at the TPC at Sawgrass, a course with an abundance of water, Steve Lowry safely negotiated the water that virtually surrounds the green on the infamous par-3 17th. With his ball safely on the back of the green, Lowry began his walk up. But before he could reach the green and mark his ball, an enterprising seagull swooped down and began pecking at his ball, picking it up and dropping it several times. Eventually the bird was successful in securing the ball, but only for a few seconds. As the bird attempted to fly off with his prize, it lost its grip again and the ball dropped into the water behind the green.

A penalty? Of course not.

The bird is considered an outside agency and, according to Rule 18.1, Lowry was able to replace his ball as close as possible to the original spot.

LOST AND FOUND

In the world of professional golf, a lost ball or the opportunity to search for and identify a ball is a rare occurrence. Seldom does a player have to tromp around in waist-deep rough looking for a golf ball. In most cases there are a sufficient number of marshals, spectators and other assorted interested personnel who are more than willing to help locate an errant shot. Seldom does a lost ball stay lost for long. And, if a ball is really lost, the pro won't even bother with a fruitless search. If a ball is so far into the bushes that finding it would prove to be a detriment, why bother? Or, worse yet, what if he finds it and thinks he can "hack" it out? The results could mean several strokes.

The rule that explains a player's options and procedures for a lost ball (or a ball out-of-bounds) is Rule 27. It is straightforward and self-explanatory, and almost everyone who plays the game learns this rule early in his golfing career. If the ball is definitely lost, play again from the spot at which the original shot was played and add a one-stroke penalty. The confusion arises when you begin to consider exactly when a ball is deemed to be lost. And then what about all these "provisional ball" stipulations: exactly when does the provisional ball become the ball in play? And while we're here, at least in the world of professional golf, let's also consider spectators, as in "outside agency." What if a player's ball "finds" its way into the pocket of a souvenir-seeking onlooker?

Since there are a limited number of lost balls in professional and high level amateur golf, this section will not be extensive. What you'll find is a sampling of various cases that have occurred.

When can you hit three balls from the tee (discounting mulligans) and still only lie three when the third tee shot has come to rest? In a major championship, of course. Majors just seem to produce the peculiar situations.

In the 1998 U.S. Open, mini-tour player Chris Kaufman was involved in a "lost it, found it" ruling that eventually resulted in his missing the cut by just a few shots. On the par-3 15th Kaufman pushed his tee shot and the ball ricocheted off a tree and headed toward lost and found territory or possibly out-of-bounds. He then played a provisional ball in case the original could not be found. The provisional went right down the middle of the fairway.

But bad news was waiting. Kaufman found the original ball situated in a dark and dreadful lie, virtually unplayable. He then questioned the rules official assigned to the group concerning his options. They were threefold, all involving a one-stroke penalty for an unplayable lie: take two club-lengths relief not nearer the hole (an unusable option being deep in the woods); keep the point where the ball now lay between him and the hole and go back as far as he wished (an even worse suggestion); or return to the tee.

But Kaufman thought there might be one more option: play the provisional. Not in this case. The official correctly informed him that once the original ball was located the provisional ball had to be abandoned.

Kaufman returned to the tee to play for the third time. Since the provisional ball had no effect on his stroke total, he would be playing his third shot, which included a one-stroke penalty for the unplayable lie.

Golf enthusiasts are like all other sports fans, they like to collect souvenirs, especially original ones from an event they have attended. But, unlike baseball, spectators at golf events are not allowed to keep the foul balls. In fact, there's even a term in the rulebook for spectators—outside agency. Try using that term next time you attend a golf tournament. Someone will likely fit you with a blue blazer and a tie and make you walk the course in the middle of June. Yet, despite the prohibition for spectators to become involved in the play of the game, it does happen. A well-meaning observer may become a hungry souvenir-hound and pocket a golf ball when he thinks no one is looking.

There are a couple of cases from the 1998 U.S. Open in which this situation arose, one with an acceptable result and the other with an unfortunate conclusion.

On one hole Jeff Maggert pushed his tee shot into the trees and it was "apprehended" by a fan. Fortunately the rules do not require the next shot to be played from the fan's pocket while he is still wearing the pants. In this case the rules official used his best judgment to assist Maggert in determining where the ball most likely would have finished but for the interference. There is no penalty involved.

An almost identical incident befell amateur Paul Simson on the 10th. Simson hooked his tee shot into the trees on the left and the ball was quickly requisitioned by a spectator who then fled the scene of the crime. Unfortunately for Simson, there was no rules official or observer at the scene to assist him with his options. Simson couldn't find his ball. Not surprising since his gallery of one had gone off with it. He assumed the ball was lost and thus continued under the lost ball rule, returning to the tee and playing his third shot. The great tragedy is that the stroke and distance penalty cost him a chance to play on the weekend. He missed the cut by one shot.

———————

Rule 28 (Ball Unplayable) explains a player's options and procedures if he chooses to declare his ball unplayable. How does this enter into our chapter on Lost and Found? Quite simply, you must positively identify your ball before you can declare it unplayable. Therefore, if you think your ball is stuck in a tree, you must positively identify it; otherwise it's considered a lost ball. The good news is that you can be quite creative in your identification process. For instance, you can climb the tree ala Nick Faldo at the 13th several years ago at the Pebble Beach Pro-Am. The rules even permit you to use binoculars (Decision 27/14).

This, quite expectedly, brings us to Jose Maria Olazábal playing in the

Tournament Players Championship a few years ago. His tee shot on the 10th hole was a push-fade that tangled with a tree. Hundreds of spectators witnessed the fact that the ball had indeed struck the tree, but not one of them could attest that the ball had bounced away. Conclusion: the ball must still be in the tree. Olazábal and a rules official could even see a ball up in the tree. Both deduced that it was Olazábal's ball, so the official permitted him to take an unplayable lie. Wrong decision! The ball was never positively identified and Olazábal should have continued play as if the ball was lost.

This ruling had an effect on another situation at the TPC in 1999. Nick Faldo was disqualified from the event for signing an inaccurate scorecard that resulted from an incorrect procedure concerning a lost ball or an unplayable lie. Faldo had hit a shot that was "obviously" stuck in a tree. Both he and playing partner Corey Pavin could see the ball. Pavin, having knowledge of the Olazábal incident, advised Faldo that he could declare the ball unplayable. Once again, the wrong advice. When the details of the situation came out, Faldo had already signed his scorecard and was consequently disqualified.

———————————

Let's offer a rhetorical question. How important is it to properly identify your ball before playing another golf shot? Obvious answer: Very. Failure to properly identifying your ball usually results in a two-stroke penalty for playing a wrong ball (Rule 15.3). However, the following illustration demonstrates quite effectively how one's failure to identifying his ball can expand into a golfing catastrophe. Try to follow along.

Duke University was engaged in a fierce battle with rival Wake Forest for a college tournament championship. One of the Blue Devils came to the final hole needing only a par-4 for a fine 69 that would put Duke in the lead. Unfortunately, his drive sailed into the woods, but wisely he played a provisional ball—just in case. After searching for three minutes he found a ball that he believed to be his, same make and same number. From there he played to the green, picking up his provisional along the way. But when he got to the green and marked his ball, he noticed that it did not have two blue dots on it, which was his personal identification mark. He knew immediately he had a formidable problem.

He called for a rules official to help sort out the situation. The bad news was that he had already played a wrong ball, which requires a two-stroke penalty. The good news was that he still had two minutes remaining to find his original ball. That extra two-minute search produced nothing. With the original ball lost, the provisional now became the ball in play. Since he had already picked it up, he was assessed a one-stroke penalty for lifting a ball in play, Rule 18.2, and the ball had to be replaced. He then finished the hole in three more strokes.

Now it was time to add it up. Regrettably, no accountants were on the scene. Tee shot—that's one; lost ball and plays the provisional—lies three; lifting a ball in play—now it's four; three more strokes to finish the hole—a grand total of seven. Then add the two-stroke penalty for playing a wrong ball. The total equals nine! So, instead of an excellent 69, the final score was a respectable 74. You can probably surmise the final result of the tournament: Wake Forest won by a single stroke.

IT'S HAZARDOUS

Hazards present unique and challenging situations in the game of golf in both the playing of the game and the application of the rules. They come in two varieties: bunkers and water hazards. Bunkers are usually some sort of hollow or depression that is filled with sand or the like. The non-technical definition of a water hazard is what you might expect, except that it does not necessarily need to be filled with water. Water hazards are of two types—regular water hazards and lateral water hazards—depending on their position on the golf course. Water hazards are marked by yellow lines or stakes and lateral water hazards are indicated by red lines or stakes.

Both strike fear into the heart of the amateur, but for the professional only the liquid variety is a cause for concern. The rules for play from a bunker are really quite fundamental, so basic in fact that they do not even warrant their own section of the rulebook. But this simplicity does not mean a lack of potential rule skirmishes. Despite their skill in playing from bunkers, touring professionals regularly incur penalties due to their actions. The rules applicable to water hazards can present a maze of confusion. The options for play or relief from water hazards are delineated in Rule 26. Even though it covers only about two pages in the rulebook, it annually presents us with several player miscues. Most players have a foundational knowledge of the rules concerning hazards. It's just the application of that knowledge in a high-pressure situation that presents a problem.

———————

Karrie Webb is a superstar on the LPGA Tour and a fiery competitor with a constantly composed demeanor. In spite of that fact, in two consecutive years Webb ran afoul of the rules regarding each variety of hazard. In one incident she was still able to prevail and win the tournament. In the other it cost her the championship.

During the 1999 Office Depot Classic, Webb drove her ball to the right of the 17th fairway into a muddy area within the confines of a lateral water hazard. In an uncustomary mental lapse she rested the head of her 6-iron on the ground inside the red hazard line. Immediately she realized her mistake and withdrew the club. Too late. The offending deed had been done and she was assessed two strokes for grounding her club in a hazard.

"I just wasn't thinking. It was a mental error," she explained later.

Fortunately, LPGA rules official Jane Reynolds met Webb in the scoring tent to prevent any scorecard errors. Reynolds commiserated, "We hate to see things like that happen. I'm sure she didn't intend to do it. Unfortunately, intent is not part of the rules."

Nevertheless, Webb persevered and went on to win the tournament.

———————

One year later in the 2000 First Star Classic, Webb again was the victim of an infraction in a hazard. This time it was in a bunker and it was not an inadvertent act. On the eighth hole of the final round she irascibly hit the sand with her club after failing to extricate her ball on the first attempt. That's considered grounding your club in a hazard and carries a two-stroke penalty.

Unfortunately this time she was not able to regroup. She lost the tournament by one stroke.

———————

"It's Hazardous" has proven to be more than just a trite phrase for Sweden's Thomas Bjorn. Sand proved to be his undoing during the 2003 British Open and eventually cost him the championship. Bjorn was leading the tournament by two strokes with just four holes remaining when he met a sandy demise. Most ardent golf fans are aware that Bjorn required three strokes to extricate his ball from a greenside bunker on the par-3 16th at Royal St. George's Golf Club during the final round. All this led to a double-bogey at a time when he was leading the tournament by two shots and looking like the first Swedish champion in the event's history. Add this to the fact that Bjorn had made bogey on the previous hole when his tee shot found a fairway bunker and you have a sandy demise when a major championship was on the line.

At the end of 72 holes, Bjorn had lost The Open to American Ben Curtis by one stroke. But, despite his troubles at the 15th and 16th on the final day, it was a bunker incident on the first day of play that also contributed greatly to the final outcome.

Bjorn was playing steadily on the first day of the tournament when he arrived at the 17th hole. His tee shot found a fairway bunker and when he attempted to play his shot to the green from it, he failed to clear the lip and the ball remained in the bunker. In a fit of frustration Bjorn took a swipe at the sand with his club. Immediately realizing his breach of Rule 13.4, he called the two-stroke penalty on himself and finished the hole with a quadruple bogey. Those two wasted strokes eventually cost him the championship.

Incurring a penalty due to frustration or anger is one matter, but when you incur penalty strokes because you are not aware of your options, especially when you're playing the game for a living, it is an unforgivable sin. This is particularly true when it is a basic procedure like Rule 28 (Ball Unplayable).

Jill Briles-Hinton presents us with an excellent case in point. Playing in the first round of the Palm Beach National Pro-Am not too long ago, one of Jill's tee shots found a fairway bunker. The lie in the bunker was not to her liking so she declared the ball unplayable, which is a legal option. However, when she took her drop from the bunker she did so outside the bunker. That procedure is incorrect. Rule 28 dictates that a ball declared unplayable in a bunker must be dropped within the bunker unless you elect to return to the spot from which the original ball was played. Unfortunately for Briles-Hinton, her procedural infraction was not discovered until after she had signed her scorecard. The penalty ultimately became disqualification.

Two-shot penalties are always devastating and sometimes, when there are millions of golf fans watching, they're thoroughly embarrassing. The 2003 Masters provided us one of those rare moments when a player's ball actually comes back to strike his person.

Thirty-nine year-old Jeff Maggert had been a successful and consistent, although unspectacular, player on the PGA Tour for many years when he arrived at the 2003 Masters. But when he stepped to the tee of the third hole in the final round he was leading the tournament. The third is a short par-4 measuring approximately 350 yards. The hole demands strategy, not strength. The usual play during the Masters is an iron off the tee and then a sand wedge to an elevated green. Maggert elected to employ that strategy but hooked his two-iron into a fairway bunker. Nevertheless, his position was not all that critical. With little more than a pitching wedge remaining, he would almost surely make par and retain his lead. But the wedge was bladed ever-so-slightly into the bank of the bunker directly in front of him. The ball caromed straight back, hitting him in the chest and falling again into the bunker. The penalty: two shots. From that point Maggert made triple-bogey and essentially eliminated his chances for victory although he did rally with a couple of birdies to get within one stroke of the lead during the back nine.

Maggert's assessment of the peculiarity, "I guess my reflexes aren't what they used to be."

The Rules of Golf states that a player is within his right to play a ball from a water hazard if he so desires. This is one of his options whether the ball has finished in a water hazard or a lateral water hazard. In fact, this is such a popular option that the cover of the 2004-2005 USGA Rules book has a picture of an anonymous golfer playing from a lateral water hazard. There are just three conditions that must be met. The first states that the player cannot "test the condition of the hazard." The second, which just about every golfer knows, is that you cannot ground your club. The third forbids a player from touching or moving any loose impediment lying in or touching the hazard. It should be pointed out that these stipulations are not explained in Rule 26 (Water Hazards), but rather in Rule 13.4, which addresses playing the ball as it lies.

This short explanation leads us to Paul Azinger participating in the 1991 Doral Open in Miami played on the Blue Monster, a typical Florida golf course with lots of water. On one hole Azinger found his ball just barely submerged in a greenside water hazard and he decided to play it. In his effort to get a comfortable stance, Azinger kicked away some stones with his left foot. That's a clear violation of the rule and a two-stroke penalty.

HOW DO YOU SPELL R-E-L-I-E-F?

The big question used to be "How do you spell R-E-L-I-E-F?" But the pertinent question for golfers is "What is relief?"

"Relief Situations and Procedures" is a key subsection of the rulebook. There are nine rules in this subsection (Rules 20-28)—a rule for taking relief from practically every situation imaginable.

Taking relief from a particular situation on the golf course is not as easy as it might seem. One could argue that it is the trickiest portion of the rules. There are a multitude of questions to be answered. Do I take one club-length or two? Which way do I go—back, front, to the side? Is a penalty stroke (or strokes) involved? Am I allowed to clean the ball after I pick it up? Who can figure their way through this maze? Certainly not your average touring professional. And certainly not the club player who gets to tee it up just once or twice a week.

———————

Of course, the first question a player must ask himself is, "Do I get relief?" or in the following case, "Can I move the stake?" A moveable obstruction is a tricky deal. In fact, you better not touch it until an official is consulted.

Chip Beck was tied for the lead during the third round of the 1992 Greater Greensboro Open when he pull-hooked his tee shot on the 14th. When he found his ball it had come to rest next to an out-of-bounds stake. Without thinking, Beck pulled the stake and began to prepare for his next shot. As he stood there with stake in hand, it dawned on him that maybe he should not have removed the stake. He replaced the stake and finished out the hole with a bogey. But the deed had been done. Even the act of just pulling out the stake is an infraction. In the end he had to add two penalty strokes to that bogey giving him a triple-bogey. Eventually he finished in a tie for third, but without the penalty he would have finished in second place alone. The cost: $81,563.

Irishman Harry Bradshaw lost the 1949 British Open Championship in a playoff to Bobby Locke, but the playoff might never have happened were it not for a quirky rule situation.

While playing the par-4 fifth hole during the second round, Bradshaw's ball came to rest in a broken beer bottle. At this point you would expect Bradshaw to summon a rules official before playing his next shot. Not Bradshaw. He figured he knew how to spell R-E-L-I-E-F. N-O-N-E. Invoking the "play the ball as it lay" principle, Bradshaw grabbed his "beer & glass" iron, closed his eyes and played away. The ball advanced only about 20 yards and Bradshaw finished the hole with a six.

Should we specu-
late what the outcome
might have been had
Bradshaw called for an
official? Probably not
when you consider
that the results most
likely would be the
same. At that time un-
der the rules of golf

Bradshaw would not have been permitted to take relief from the broken beer
bottle. The evolution of the rules on obstructions, moveable or immoveable,
was slow in its progress. By the time of the 1949 British Open, it still did not
include such items as bottles. In fact, prior to 1952 the R&A adhered to the
practice of trying to define each and every item that was to be considered an
obstruction.

One way not to spell RELIEF is by removing part of a bridge. When the 1965 PGA Championship was held at Laurel Valley in Pennsylvania, Arnold Palmer was the "unofficial host" for the tournament. That's enough of a distraction even for the "King." And it apparently showed on the first hole of the championship. Palmer's second shot to the par-4 came up short left of the green and right near a temporary footbridge. Quickly, a zealous marshal removed the railings from the bridge and Palmer played his pitch onto the green and saved par. There seemed to be no problem. But just a couple of holes later Palmer was informed by an official that he was being assessed a two-stroke penalty for permitting an improvement to his line of play.

In his landmark book *The Principles Behind the Rules of Golf*, Richard Tufts states that there are two underlying principles to all of the rules of golf: 1. "You play the course as you find it;" and 2. "You put your ball in play at the start of the hole, play only your own ball and do not touch it until you lift it from the hole." All of this begs the question, "Under what extreme circumstances, if any, is a player entitled to relief?" The answer to this question is provided throughout the rules. However, certain situations arise that require the judgment of a rules official or perhaps officials.

Based on *The Rules of Golf* and Tufts' treatise, the essence and challenge of the game lies in the fact that all players must play the ball as it lies. Even a great champion such as Seve Ballesteros is not exempt from this principle. But Seve was not beneath trying to "influence" officials when he thought he might receive a ruling in his favor. Because of his stature in the game, Seve could be quite intimidating when standing in front of an official and pleading his case. However, during one memorable Masters' incident, Ballesteros met his match in the equally intimidating presence of the R&A's Michael Bonallack, the former multi-British Amateur champion.

On the par-5 13th hole of Augusta National's famous Amen Corner, Ballesteros had quite predictably hooked his tee shot in the trees on the left in an attempt to cut the corner. With no shot to the green, even for a player of Seve's ability, he desperately needed a bit of relief from a damp spot just to the left of Rae's Creek. He summoned a rules official, who, after examining the situation, decided to ask for a second opinion. Bonallack was summoned. Knowing Seve's reputation, he arrived at the scene and began to confer with the other official, but not before waving off Seve, who was anxiously waiting to give his opinion. Bonallack addressed the ball with an imaginary club, looked up at Ballesteros and declared, "Play it!"

Ballesteros grumbled his acceptance of the decision and chipped out sideways to the fairway.

Most golfers who play the game regularly are aware that they are permitted to take relief from an immovable obstruction if it interferes with their stance or swing (Rule 24.2(A)). Many may not realize that they are not allowed to stretch this rule by using an exaggerated stance or swing. Tiger Woods does.

On the 36th and final hole in the finals of the 1996 U.S. Amateur held at the Witch Hollow course at Pumpkin Ridge, Tiger's ball stopped just inches behind a small metal drain about 50 yards from the hole. But Tiger didn't call for a referee and beg for relief. Realizing that his intended shot was a pitch that would not be affected by the drain, Tiger played on. He never considered trying to stretch the rule by using an exaggerated swing or a made up shot. Tiger went on to win the championship, which was the last of his three consecutive U.S. Amateur Championships.

―――――

There are occasions when players on the professional tours get relief from situations that you would not get when playing with your Saturday morning foursome. Often these unique circumstances revolve around temporary immovable obstructions such as scoreboards or grandstands erected specially for the tournament.

At the conclusion of the 2001 NEC Invitational played at Firestone's

North Course, Tiger Woods and Jim Furyk were tied and headed into a playoff. On the third extra hole, Firestone's 18th, Woods pull-hooked his drive into a cluster of pine trees. A simple pitch back to the fairway was blocked by the trees, but Woods did have a look at the green though the shot was somewhat chancy. Plus, luck was on his side. Between his ball and the hole was a long supporting guide wire helping to support a large scoreboard.

PGA Tour official Mike Shea ruled that Woods could obtain relief because he had a "reasonable shot" and there was a "temporary immovable obstruction in a clear line between his ball and the hole."

After receiving relief, Woods bumped his ball some 50 yards from the green and eventually made par, tying Furyk on the hole. Woods ultimately won the playoff on the seventh extra hole with a birdie.

———

While the rules do allow relief from obstructions, you are not always required to take relief. If the point where you are to drop the ball is unfavorable, you may elect to play the ball from where it lies. But don't pick up the ball until you have made that decision.

Corey Pavin was well aware of this rule during the 1996 U.S. Open at Oakland Hills, Michigan where he was defending his title. On his first hole of the championship, Pavin's second shot came to rest just over the green on a cart path. Naturally he was entitled to relief. Before picking up his ball he conferred with a rules official to determine the nearest point of relief in accordance with Rule 24.2. After a short deliberation the official pointed to a spot that would produce a muddy, downhill lie. Finding that option not to his liking, Pavin elected to play the ball from the path and with great skill pitched the ball to six feet and made par.

Had Pavin picked up his ball before considering his relief point he would have been assessed a one-stroke penalty if he wanted to replace it on the path. Most likely he would have chosen to accept the muddy lie as his relief.

———

While it might not appear equitable that a player can go from a substandard situation to a favorable one, knowing this point in the rules can be extremely advantageous. Such is the case of Patty Sheehan in the 1992 U.S. Women's Open at Oakmont.

Trailing Juli Inkster by one shot on the 72nd hole, Sheehan's drive finished in the right rough. As luck would have it, they were returning from a two-hour rain delay and her ball was lying in casual water. The nearest point of relief was in the fairway. After taking relief to the fairway, she hit a 5-iron that finished 15 feet from the hole, and from there she made birdie to tie Inkster. On the next day she beat Inkster in an 18-hole playoff.

The rules of golf do not differentiate between rough and fairway. They are uniquely combined in the phrase "through the green." This encompasses everywhere on the golf course except the teeing ground, the putting green and hazards. This term, or its linguistic parent, first appeared in a rule code in 1783 and has survived in one form or another until this day.

The details of the rules can be quite confusing, especially when they involve relief procedures. Professionals often fail to differentiate Rules 24 (Immovable Obstructions) and 25 (Abnormal Ground Conditions) from Rule 26 regarding water hazards. The following two cases examine this confusion.

During the final round of the 1996 Alfred Dunhill Masters, Colin Montgomerie pulled his tee shot on the fifth hole to the left and into a drainage ditch. The ditch was marked as a water hazard so Montgomerie took the proper drop with a one-stroke penalty. After the first drop rolled back into the hazard, he redropped and the ball was in play. But before he hit his third drop, he noticed that his feet were still in the hazard. Believing that he was entitled to complete relief, Montgomerie picked up the ball and dropped again. Unfortunately Montgomerie was incorrect in his belief. The result was a two-stroke penalty: one for lifting a ball in play and another for not replacing it—Rule 18.2.

A similar situation confronted Gary Player during the 1999 Masters Tournament. Player hit his second shot on the par-5 13th into the creek that fronts the green. After taking the proper relief and a one-stroke penalty, he was about to hit his pitch when he noticed that one of his feet was still in the hazard. He quickly conferred with the Rules official, "My foot is in the hazard in order to play this shot. Does that matter?" The answer is No.

Rules 24 and 25 allow a player to take complete relief from the obstruction, moveable or immoveable, or condition that affects his swing or stance. Complete relief MUST be taken. Rule 26 delineates the procedures for dealing with relief from a water hazard (under a penalty of one-stroke), but has no reference to a player's stance.

ON THE GREEN

Without detailed consideration it would seem that once you reach the green, any confrontation with the rules would be minimal. It really sounds quite unceremonious, especially as we play today. You mark your ball with a coin or similar object, you clean your ball and then, when it's your turn to putt, you replace the ball and make your putt. But alas, as with almost everything in life and golf, it's never quite as undemanding as it seems. There was a time when you could not even mark your ball. Those were the days of the stymie. At one point in the evolution of the game, the rules stated that you were allowed to mark your ball only once. Mark it more than once and a penalty stroke was assessed.

Actually, once you finally arrive on the green, Rules 16 and 17 (The Putting Green and The Flagstick) are not the only ones that come into play. Rules 18 (Ball at Rest Moved), Rule 19 (Ball in Motion Deflected or Stopped), Rule 20 (Lifting, Dropping and Placing; Playing from Wrong Place), Rule 21 (Cleaning Ball), Rule 22 (Interfering with or Assisting Play), Rule 23 (Loose Impediments) address situations that could possibly transpire on the green.

———————

Regardless of the level of competition, even experienced professionals encounter an occasional rule situation on the green. Sometimes these circumstances are self-induced, produced by a definite lack of thinking. This following incident demonstrates why you must keep your wits about you at all times, especially on the green. It also serves to illustrate how the ritual of marking, moving and replacing your ball on the green can become complicated and appear chess-like in its procedure. It also makes you wonder what these guys are thinking about. Read slowly and try to imagine the scene.

Before there was the Nationwide Tour, there was the Buy.com Tour; and before the Buy.com Tour, there was the Nike Tour; and before the Nike Tour, there was the Hogan Tour. All this was the minor league for the PGA Tour. The play was usually quite exemplary and, like their brothers on the PGA Tour, the participants' knowledge and thinking concerning the rules was questionable.

Esteban Toledo and John Flannery were engaged in a playoff for the 1991 Ben Hogan Reno Open. When they reached the green on the third extra hole, both faced par putts along the same line. Being closest, Flannery marked his ball and then moved the marker one putterhead length to the side. Toledo putted and missed, but, instead of tapping in for his bogey, he marked his ball.

Now at this point you would figure that Flannery would be extra careful. Wrong! Flannery failed to move his marker back and putted in for what he thought was a par and victory. Wrong again! He was assessed a two-stroke penalty giving him a double-bogey six. So now you would think that Toledo would only have to tap in for his bogey five to win the tournament. Wrong for the third time! After Flannery had made his putt, Toledo's caddy had picked up his marker. Pen-

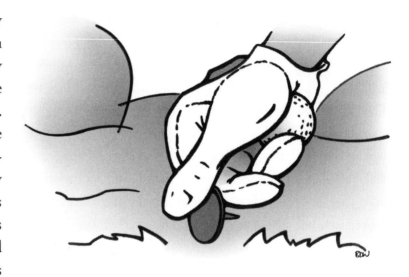

alty: one stroke and Toledo putted in for his double-bogey six. The hole was tied. Thank goodness, Flannery won on the next hole with a par.

All this business about marking your ball on the green seems straightforward. To mark the position of your ball on the green just place a coin or similar object directly behind the ball and pick it up. If your marker happens to be in another player's line, just move the marker a putterhead length or two to the left or right. When it's your turn to putt, replace the ball in front of the coin and pick up the marker, unless you have had to move it from someone's line. But apparently, even this uncomplicated ritual is occasionally too much for the pros to handle. It seems to get most confusing right at the point of moving the marker a putterhead or two and then moving it back. The difficulty is not physical. Rather the problem appears to be mental. No one remembers to move his marker back.

South African Bobby Locke gained a reputation as one of the greatest putters of his time and perhaps of all time. But even a player of his great skill and touch on the greens can run afoul of the rules.

The 1957 British Open began with an unusual change of venue for the championship and ended with a most bizarre and perhaps controversial ruling on the last green. The Championship was originally scheduled to be played at Muirfield but was switched at the last moment due to politics in Egypt. When Colonel Nasser nationalized the Suez Canal Company, it set off a political chain reaction that eventually had ramifications in the golf world. Nasser's actions caused Britain and France to invade Egypt, which in turn caused a shortage of oil, which caused fuel rationing. Because of Muirfield's somewhat remote location, R&A officials felt that it might be difficult for participants and spectators to reach the course. The tournament was thus switched to St. Andrews.

This was also the first championship in which the leaders were sent out last, which led to the drama on the final green. Locke arrived at the 18th hole of the final round with a three-stroke lead on his closest competitor and playing partner, Peter Thomson. Thomson was trying for his fourth straight British Open victory, but it was not to be. Even the officials saw to that. When Locke's second shot on the 72nd hole finished just three feet from the hole, it almost assured him of victory. But one more formality remained.

Locke's ball was directly on Thomson's line, so, as the rules allowed, he marked it one putterhead length to the side. But, when it was his turn to putt, he replaced the ball at the marker and putted out. He had failed to return the ball to its original position. Oddly, in all the excitement no one immediately noticed. Even if they had, there was no rule in force at the time except for disqualification at the committee's discretion. When the mishap was finally brought to the committee's attention, they ruled that Locke had not profited from the situation and allowed his birdie and final score to remain. Even under today's rules (20.7) with the applicable two-stroke penalty, he would still have prevailed by a single stroke if the oversight had been noticed before he signed his scorecard.

In the 1997 Mercedes Championship, David Ogrin had a momentary lapse of memory but a spectator did not. Ogrin forgot to return his marker to its original position on the 14th green of the final round and playing partner Tiger Woods failed to notice the mistake. Ogrin signed his card and thought nothing further about the matter. Sometime later a spectator informed a tournament official what had happened, who in turn informed Ogrin, who then realized it was a disqualification situation.

It's a two-stroke penalty for failing to return one's marker to its original position, but if you don't include that on your scorecard before you sign it, it's a disqualification. Ogrin was down the road.

———————

Perhaps the order of the putting ritual becomes a bit complicated, especially under the pressure of the final hole of a championship despite the fact that it has been rehearsed and put into practice thousands of times.

The distinguished German golfer Bernhard Langer has a reputation for being meticulous and orderly on the golf course. Seldom, if ever, does Langer make a mental mistake while playing. But even the presumably invincible succumb to the intense pressure of tournament golf and eventually the rules.

During the Greg Norman Holden International in 1999, Langer arrived at the final hole needing only a par on the 225-yard par-3 to claim his first victory in nearly two years. Langer's tee shot drifted right into a greenside bunker and plugged. He blasted over the green and then chipped to about 10 feet. Now he needed to make the bogey putt to tie. Langer marked his ball and waited. But when it was his turn, he unexplainably picked up his marker before replacing his ball. The resulting one-stroke penalty and the two putts gave him a triple-bogey for the hole and no championship.

Composed as always, Langer remarked, "I don't know, I just picked it up. It's never happened before and it happened today. I didn't do it on purpose, it just happened."

———————————

There are times when one is sent into serious contemplation as to just what the touring professionals of the world are visualizing when a situation arises that could possibly be construed as a rule infraction or procedural question. When thousands or tens of thousands or even hundreds of thousands of dollars are at stake, why would they not ask for guidance before signing their scorecards? If penalty strokes are to be added because of an infraction, once the scorecard is signed, it's too late. Is it ignorance, misunderstanding or overconfidence?

During a recent Tournament Players Championship at TPC Sawgrass, Davis Love III had successfully negotiated his tee shot on the infamous island green 17th. But in taking his practice stroke in preparation for his birdie putt, Love accidentally hit his ball. Then, instead of returning his ball to its original position and adding a one-stroke penalty, he played it from the new position. That's a two-stroke penalty (see Rule 18.2(A)).

Love then played 18, went to the scorer's tent and signed his card. He said not a word about the incident.

Now the real question is why did not Love or playing partner Justin Leonard double check with the officials to insure the correct penalty had been assessed? One suspects that Love and Leonard thought there was no penalty involved, just play the ball from the new position and add one for the mistaken hit.

Of course, once the PGA Tour Rules Committee discovered the error, it was too late. Disqualification at a cost of over $105,000.

You don't want to move the ball back to its former position if it has moved on its own. It doesn't matter how—gravity, gust of wind, earthquake, whatever.

John Daly encountered this circumstance during the first round of the 1996 U.S. Open at Oakland Hills, Michigan. On the fourth green Daly was facing a downhill 20-footer. As he stepped over the ball, Daly stopped abruptly.

Quickly calling for the official, he explained the problem, "My ball moved!"

The official was quick to analyze the situation, "Did you address the ball?"

(addressing the ball means taking your stance and grounding your club).

Daly confirmed, "No."

"Then there's no problem," replied the official. "Play away."

The following incident is open to several categories within this volume. It could have been included with Knowledge, Honesty or even Rules Officials and Interpretation because the actions of the rules officials could possibly have influenced the actions of the player involved as well as other players on the course. However, we have placed it here because it helps to prove our point that life on the green is more complicated than it might first appear. This incident is also directly tied to another involving Sophie Gustafson that you will find in the chapter on Rules Officials and Interpretation.

When Gustafson became victorious in the 2003 Samsung World Championship she had to endure a pair of rulings before signing her scorecard. By the time Gustafson had reached the 14th green she was the leader of the tournament despite starting the day five shots out of the lead. Her approach to the 14th had left her some 30 feet from the hole, but the ball was clinging precariously to the side of a slope. Gustafson marked her ball and waited her turn (fortunately her coin did not slide down the slope). When her turn arrived, she gingerly replaced her ball and lined up the putt. As she addressed the ball, or what appeared to be that action, the ball began to move and rolled down the slope an additional 20 feet away.

This is where the debate began and the instant replay from every possible angle kicked in. Television announcers, after reviewing an infinite number of replays, were adamant in their conclusion that Gustafson had soled her putter and thus addressed the ball, requiring a one-stroke penalty.

For her part Gustafson never flinched in her reaction or wavered from her description of the situation. She was persistent in her assessment that she had not grounded her putter, insisting that she was well aware of the precarious position of the ball and the penalty that was involved.

LPGA rules officials assessed the happenings in the most detailed manner, viewing instant replays and interviewing players and caddies. In the end they sustained the integrity of the player. It is worth noting that although the television announcers were suspect of Gustafson's story, all the players that could have possibly been affected by the decision were totally supportive of Gustafson and the LPGA officials.

There is a further disturbing footnote to this incident. While it may be acceptable for the instant replay to assist in the decision-making process, the medium of television was used as an opinion-shaping mechanism. Two former touring pros turned television commentators called into question the integrity of the player and ultimately the spirit of the game. These announcers attempted to become judge and jury for all involved. Fortunately, their conclusion of the situation was not sought.

The Seve Cup is an international competition between teams from Great Britain/Ireland and Continental Europe that has a similar format to the Ryder Cup and President's Cup. The matches were conceived and inaugurated by Seve Ballesteros, Spain's greatest golfer. All of the competition is conducted at Match Play, a form of competition that touring professionals do not engage in very often. Rules under the Match Play format differ at several junctures; however, rules governing conduct on The Putting Green (Rule 16) are identical except for the penalty for breach of the rule. It was a controversy under this rule which arose in the 2003 version of the Seve Cup.

The difference of opinion arose during the singles match between Ireland's Padraig Harrington and Spain's Jose Maria Olazábal. Both players reached the par-5 third in three with Harrington at 10 feet and Olazábal at eight feet. Olazábal arrived at the green first and began to repair what he believed to be pitch marks in his line. When Harrington arrived, he questioned whether or not the marks were ball marks and asked Olazábal not to repair them. Olazábal paid no attention and continued his gardening. Harrington appealed to referee Tony Gray. But by the time Gray arrived at the green, the marks had been repaired and he was unable to make a judgment. Believing his integrity was in question, Olazábal conceded the hole. The match went to the 18th hole where Harrington sank a three-foot putt for a halve, clinching the Cup for Great Britain/Ireland 15-13. Without the incident on the third green, we will never know if the outcome may have been different. What we do know is that the relationship between two good friends sustained great damage.

One of the cardinal rules of behavior on the green is that you cannot touch the line of your putt unless you are repairing a ball mark. The following incident illustrates an infrequent occurrence but also demonstrates the details of the rules.

During a recent One-2-One British Masters, former Ryder Cup golfer Howard Clark was penalized two strokes for repairing a damaged hole. This falls under Rule 16.1(A), touching the line of a putt on the putting green. The edge of the hole is considered part of the line of a putt (Decision 16-1a/5). Since the damage had apparently not been caused by a golf ball, this was a violation of the rule and Clark incurred a penalty.

Clark's biggest blunder may not have been his repair of the hole, but his failure to confer with a rules official. In the unlikely case that one could not have been reached he would have been permitted to repair the hole if it absolutely needed major repairs.

———————

Just what can you do if you have a little sand or dirt between your ball and the hole? Certainly you can brush it away. But until a rule change that took effect in 2004, you could only brush it away with your hand or your putter. With the advent of the change for 2004 the player is now permitted to remove loose impediments on the green "by any means, provided he does not press anything down." This change will definitely be a great assistance in preventing absentminded penalties.

This stipulation of only using your hand or your putter to brush away loose impediments brought about a number of annual violations prior to the change, mostly due to ignorance. In the 2003 Wachovia Championship Vijay Singh walked onto the fourth green in the first round and promptly brushed away some sand with his towel. Fellow competitor Brad Faxon knew this was a violation and brought it to Singh's attention. Singh hailed a rules official who confirmed a violation of Rule 16.1(A)(8). Singh even requested to see the rule in black and white to which he presumably replied, "That's a stupid rule."

But Singh has other peers who have also violated this rule. In the 1999 Phoenix Open, Jesper Parnevik was disobedient of this rule when he used his glove to clean away some loose impediments.

THE SCORECARD

While it does not directly influence the actual playing of the game, the ritual of signing the scorecard has had a direct effect on the results of a surprising number of tournaments through the years. In this section we will examine situations where players have signed an incorrect scorecard. We will not consider those who have been disqualified due to a penalty assessed after the scorecard was signed. Disqualification in these cases was a consequential effect of another rule violation.

Every year on the professional tours of the world there are numerous disqualifications following the return of an incorrect scorecard by a player.

Rule 6.6 gives the requirements on presenting the scorecard to the committee following a player's round. There are two ways for a player to be disqualified after he has returned his scorecard. First, if he simply fails to sign the card, he is disqualified. Second, if he signs for a score lower than that which he actually played to. This pertains to the hole-by-hole score, not the total. A player is not responsible for his arithmetic. All he needs to verify is that his score for each individual hole is correct.

The signing of an incorrect scorecard is usually a highly publicized incident. The high frequency of this mental lapse is alarming. The only reasonable explanation for such an error would be the combination of the pressure of the tournament and the excitement of the moment. These two factors joined together override rational thinking at exactly the wrong moment. As you might expect, major championships and other high-pressure tournaments such as qualifying schools have a high frequency of scorecard mishaps. The results of such a mistake are often disastrous.

To reemphasize the fact that the rules do not require a player to be a skilled mathematician, we present the following case. Remember, a player is only responsible for his score on each individual hole and not the resulting arithmetic at the end of the line.

The excitement of playing well in a major championship affects even the most seasoned veteran. In the first round of the 1960 PGA Championship held at Firestone Country Club in Akron, Ohio, Sam Snead shot a two-under-par-68, which put him one shot behind leader Arnold Palmer. But Snead had signed for a 69, which playing partner Don January had written as the total. Snead had verified that the score for each individual hole was correct, but in his excitement had not noticed January's mistake in arithmetic. A correction of the error was made and Snead's 68 stood as the proper score.

———————

When a player returns an incorrect scorecard after any round of a tournament, it is a distressing moment, not to mention potentially expensive. But when an incorrect card is discovered following the final round of a major championship, it is disastrous. This situation has occurred twice since competition began in the major championships with the inaugural British Open in 1860.

Undoubtedly the most heartbreaking and most publicized scorecard error occurred following the final round of the 1968 Masters. For 72 holes Roberto de Vicenzo and Bob Goalby had battled for the Masters title. When all the players had completed their rounds, there appeared to be a tie between Goalby and de Vicenzo. But before long the television announcers began to show confusion, indicating there

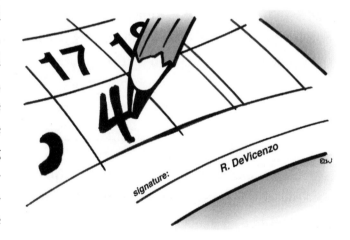

might be a problem with the scorecard of de Vicenzo. Soon it was learned that the congenial Argentinian had signed an incorrect scorecard. The consequences were gradually being understood. De Vicenzo had actually shot a magnificent final round 65 to tie Goalby. However, when he signed his card he had not noticed that his fellow-competitor and marker, Tommy Aaron, had recorded a par-4 on the 17th instead of the birdie-three he had really made. He had signed for a score higher than he had actually made and was stuck with a 66, handing the title to Goalby. When asked about the horrible oversight, de Vicenzo voiced the immortal words: "What a stupid I am."

———————

Innovation or change at the USGA, golf's ruling body in the United States, usually comes very slowly. In the following situation it was the tragedy of a major championship being snatched away because of an incorrect scorecard—a situation that probably could have been prevented—that led to a procedural change.

Having played brilliant golf in the 1957 U.S. Women's Open at Winged Foot in New York, Jackie Pung, a Chinese-American, appeared to be the winner. Pung had finished with a lower score than Betsy Rawls, a most rewarding result given the fact that she had lost to Rawls in 1953 in a playoff. In the excitement she was immediately mobbed by a multitude of family and fans. However, 40 minutes after she had apparently secured victory, it was announced that she had signed an incorrect scorecard and had been disqualified. In error she had signed for a five on the fourth hole, not the six she had played.

Why it had taken 40 minutes to discover the error is apparent in the circumstances surrounding the situation. There was no scoring tent at the time and in the thrill of the moment, she had quickly signed the card and made the unfortunate error. The penalty for signing for a score lower than actually played to is disqualification. Rawls became the champion. Following this most unfortunate incident, the USGA instituted scoring tents for the competitors.

Ironically, Rawls, who not only had a great playing career, has a masterful command of the rules of golf and was the first woman to serve on the Rules Committee for the Men's U.S. Open.

––––––

There is no doubt that the world of professional golf is a high-pressure arena. That would be a great understatement. And when you incorporate the backdrop of a major championship the pressure is even greater. But perhaps the most pressure-packed tournament in all of professional golf is the PGA Tour's qualifying school. If one has no previous exemption, a player must go through a local qualifier, then a regional qualifier just to arrive at the 108-hole final qualifying stage. Out of the thousands who begin this marathon every year, only a limited number gain a full exemption to the PGA Tour. The keen observer would wonder why anyone would make a mistake on his scorecard. Pressure does funny things to the psyche.

Enter one Jaxon Brigman, a journeyman professional trying to make it to the "big" tour. During the final round of the 1999 Qualifying School Tournament, Brigman shot a 65 to tie for the last exempt spot on the PGA Tour. However, as in the de Vicenzo case, he signed for an incorrect scorecard. His marker had mistakenly given him a four on a hole where he really made three. The 66 that he signed for had to stand. He missed his card by one stroke.

Failure to sign one's scorecard is just as bad as signing an incorrect one. Perhaps it is an even more grievous mistake, since every player knows that the scorecard must be signed to make the round official. Consider Padraig Harrington, who was leading the 2000 Benson and Hedges International Open at The Belfry, home to several Ryder Cup matches. After three rounds Harrington had built a five-stroke margin. He never got to play the final round. He was disqualified following the third round for failing to sign his scorecard after the first round. The oversight was discovered only because his hotel asked for copies of the scorecards from the first three rounds. It was then that the missing signature from the first round scorecard was detected.

———

Do you think that Harrington is alone in his oversight? Hardly! Others have gone before him. After two rounds of the 1983 Boston Five Classic, Debby Miesterlin was obviously in good spirits being near the top of the leaderboard. She was feeling very amiable. It was autographs for everyone. Everyone, that is, except Chris Johnson, who held her scorecard. Penalty: disqualification.

———

This incident has been placed last in the chapter because it made the most noise, partly because of the age in which we live where all news is global and partly because it emphasizes the need for a rule change, especially at the top levels of the game.

The 2003 British Open conducted on the Royal St. George's course in Sandwich, England, provided the annals of golf history with some interesting tales. The tournament provided us with illustrations why the game of golf can run the gamut of one's emotions. In this one tournament the golf world witnessed both a most heartwarming victory and a most heartbreaking rules incident.

The biggest story was the man who was victorious and became "The Champion Golfer for the Year," Ben Curtis. At the time of his victory Curtis was the 396th ranked player in the world and participating in his first professional major championship (see an entry on Ben Curtis in the chapter on Honesty to make this victory even more notable).

The heartbreak was provided by Rule 6.6, another inadvertent scorecard calamity that led to disaster. The summary of the incident is simple: At the end of the third round of the championship, both Mark Roe and Jesper Parnevick were disqualified for signing incorrect scorecards. The details of the incident are much more involved. The pair had forgotten to exchange scorecards on the first tee. The result at the end of 18 holes was that Roe's score was written on the card with Parnevick's name and vice versa. The tragedy is that Roe had fired a four-under par 67 and moved to one-over for the tourna-

ment and into contention, just two strokes behind the third-round leader Thomas Bjorn.

Both Roe and Parnevick signed the wrong scorecards despite several "checks and balances" that were in place by the R&A. Roe, quite naturally, was quite methodical in checking his card. Both players had their scores checked by the scorer with their group and two R&A officials. No one caught the mistake. Oddly, Australian Stuart Appleby and Phillip Price of Wales almost met with the same destiny. They were about to sign their cards and turn them in when Appleby decided to make one final, quick check. It was only then he noticed that the pair had also failed to exchange scorecards.

There was nothing that could be done to alter the situation according to R&A Officials. The rules of golf are quite explicit. A player is responsible for the correctness of *his* scorecard when he finishes the round. Peter Dawson, secretary of the R&A, was apologetic but unrelenting. "It's one of the great tragedies of championship golf," he said. "Our checking procedures have clearly failed and we take some blame, but not responsibility." As you might expect, Roe did not back down from his responsibility, "I've played golf for long enough as a professional and this mistake has never happened before. I've abided by the rules for my whole career. I accept the blame."

But (and this is with a capital "B"), could the R&A have waived off the disqualification? The answer is "Yes!" As the rule-making body and the local committee for this event, they could have stepped in and saved the situation. In fact, they had already established precedence for waiving the rules under unusual circumstances. In the 1957 British Open Bobby Locke had failed to replace his ball at the original spot on the final green before he knocked in the winning putt (for details on this incident see the entry on Bobby Locke in the chapter on On the Green—see page153). Yet, R&A officials in 2003 remained steadfast in their decision.

As you might expect, the Monday morning review began early Monday morning. The R&A promised to review its procedures for the complete scorecard process from the time a player receives his card until he signs it and turns it in.

David Rickman, rules secretary, said: "I'm sure there will be an extensive review of procedures in the recorder's hut. We thought we had a failsafe procedure, but obviously we did not. And the great sadness is that the penalty is as severe as it is. But, having said that, I sense that a rule change as such is not the answer here. I don't think there is a quick fix. Certainly in the agreed rules changes to be announced in 2004 there is no change to Rule 6, which determines a player's responsibilities."

True to their word, when the 30th edition of *The Rules of Golf* was published, there was no change to Rule 6. The question now remains, how many more tragic scorecard errors will it take to force the USGA and the R&A into finally changing the rule?

RULES OFFICIALS AND INTERPRETATION

On the surface, golf doesn't look like other sports in the manner in which the rules are applied during the playing of the game. In all other major sports, rules officials make immediate judgment calls based on the actions and reactions of the players. Infractions of the rules are penalized immediately and the play of the game continues directly, affected by the judgment call of the official. The referee must do the best that he can in a fast action situation. Usually there's no turning back except in the case of football's instant replay review scenario.

Application of the rules in golf does not involve instantaneous judgment calls. Rather, a rules official, when called to the scene of a controversy, will make an interpretation of the appropriate rule or rules based on the circumstances. Each occurrence is evaluated based upon its unique situation. The interpretation and the resulting decision should be correct. The rules official has ample time and no great sense of urgency to make the call until he is sure that it is right. Yet we can still raise a few questions about decisions that rules officials have made. In this section we'll do just that, trying to conjure up a few thoughts that perhaps the official failed to take into consideration.

The path that leads to the correct application and interpretation of the rules is littered with interpretive landmines. The small paperback booklet that fits in your back pocket is highly expandable. The 100 or so pages of rules and appendices enlarge to several hundred pages of decisions.

In its school for the training of PGA professionals, the PGA's Golf Professional Training Program requires one seminar on the rules of golf. This course, however, is basic in content dealing with everyday and common rules situations. If you want to be a certified rules official, you must attend several levels of USGA Rule Seminars, acquire hands-on experience and finally deal with genuinely unique situations.

———————

One would think that the routine actions in golf, such as marking your ball on the green, would be rather straightforward and present little or no interaction with the rules. This is not always the case.

The USGA held the 1996 U.S. Open at Oakland Hills, a somewhat hilly, tree-lined course just outside Detroit, Michigan. During one of the early rounds, Kevin Sutherland hit his second shot on the 11th hole to about 10 feet. As he approached the ball with coin in hand, intending to mark, lift and clean it, he dropped the coin, which hit the ball, moving it about four feet in the direction of the hole.

Rule 18.2 states that there is a one-stroke penalty if a player's equipment moves the ball. However, there is a caveat to this rule. Rule 20.1 provides for no penalty if the ball is moved in the process of marking it. Since Sutherland's arm was extended he was considered to be in the process of marking his ball. All he had to do was place the ball back in its original position.

Did you ever wonder why tour players so frequently call for assistance on an apparently fundamental rules situation? Part of the answer may lie in the following two examples. There is a safety factor involved. If a player proceeds on his own and commits an infraction, he will be penalized or perhaps even disqualified if the error is not caught until after he signs his scorecard. However, if he proceeds under the guidance of an official and the official makes a mistake, the player will be absolved.

Several years ago during the Masters, Scott Simpson received a favorable ruling concerning relief from a water hazard. The official with Simpson's group based his decision on a case involving Colin Montgomerie (see Chapter on R-E-L-I-E-F). The ruling turned out to be incorrect. In the process of taking a drop from a water hazard, Simpson's ball came to rest in such a position that while the ball was outside the hazard, his feet were still inside the hazard. Based on the facts of the Montgomerie case, the official believed that Simpson was entitled to relief that also included his stance. Simpson then redropped, this time ensuring that his stance was clear of the hazard. Although the ruling was incorrect, Simpson was not penalized because he had followed the directions of an official.

To the official's credit, he contacted Simpson at the 18th hole and informed him that he had received an incorrect ruling and in the future he should be aware that he is not entitled to relief from stance interference when dropping from a water hazard.

In the 2003 President's Cup held in George, South Africa, there was a brief but interesting rule incident during an alternate-shot match between Tiger Woods and Charles Howell III against Stuart Appleby and K.J. Choi.

Because of an official's mistake Appleby and Choi were absolved from a loss-of-hole penalty when they hit out of turn on the par-5 fifth hole.

It happened like this: Choi played the tee shot, but hit it so far it went through the fairway and under a small scrub. Appleby, who was scheduled to hit the next shot, decided to take an unplayable lie, which would mean the team would then be playing their third shot. In circumstances where there was no penalty involved, Choi should have played the third shot.

A rules official, Theo Manyama from the Sunshine Tour, was summoned to assist with the situation. Manyama had Choi take the drop and play the shot. Appleby figured this was correct, assuming that the penalty shot accounted for his turn. Woods and Howell immediately questioned the decision. Why was Choi playing again? As it turns out, they were right! Appleby should have played the shot even after the penalty was applied. Manyama actually knew the rule, and was in his mind making the correct decision. His mistake resulted from the fact that he thought Appleby had hit the tee shot. In short, he wasn't paying attention.

According to the rules, Appleby and Choi should have forfeited the hole for hitting out of turn. However, since the infraction had been dictated by an official they were spared the penalty.

Understandably, the whole situation was quite embarrassing for Manyama. Fortunately, he was spared further embarrassment when Woods and Howell won the hole outright, making the mistake meaningless.

———————

How complicated can getting relief from a cart path be? Find the nearest point of relief, take the allowed club-length to get a free swing and stance, drop the ball not nearer the hole and play on. Well, it's not that simple. And when it gets complicated, even a member of the PGA Rules Committee can get a little off-track.

In the first round of the 1998 PGA Championship at Seattle's Sahalee Country Club, Olin Browne's tee shot faded right and came to rest on the cart path on the right side. The official on duty, Dean Alexander, guided

Browne through the relief process. Since a cart path is an immovable obstruction, Rule 24.3 was in effect. The player must find his nearest point of relief using the club with which he will probably play his next shot and drop the ball within one club-length of the point not nearer the hole.

Alexander allowed Browne to find the nearest point of relief and then measure one driver's length backward to get more room to play. After two unsuccessful drops where the ball failed to stay within the two club-length limit, Browne tried to place the ball. He had no success here either, since the gallery had worn the area nearly bare.

At this point the procedure became quite complex even for the rules official. Rule 20.3(D) provides the procedure for a ball that will not stay at rest when placed. If not in a hazard, place the ball at the nearest spot not nearer the hole. But the only place that Browne could get the ball to remain stationary without rolling several yards was an inch or two in front of the point where the ball hit the ground on the second drop.

Since this spot was behind where the ball lay originally, Alexander allowed Browne to place it there. This turned out to be incorrect. After proceeding under Rule 24.2 and dropping twice, the correct procedure would have been to proceed under Rule 20.3(D) using the

point where the ball struck the ground as the new reference point.

Had Browne interpreted the rule himself and proceeded without a rules official, he would have been charged with playing from the wrong place and been penalized. However, since a rules official was present and guided Browne through the process, no penalty was assessed.

The arena of the PGA Tour sometimes provides circumstances for a creative interpretation of the rules. Situations that would have a different outcome in everyday play can be "stretched" because of the showcase in which the pros play.

During the final round of the 1999 Phoenix Open, Tiger Woods' tee shot on the 585-yard par-5 13th came to rest in a natural desert area to the left of the fairway. Directly in front of his ball was a chest-high decorative rock weighing about 1,000 pounds (estimates have varied greatly concerning the weight and size of the boulder). Fortunately for Woods, stones are considered loose impediments. The interfering boulder was deemed such by rules official Orlando Pope, who took into account the fact that it was not "solidly embedded" and thus could be moved.

Only one problem remained for Woods: How to move 1,000 pounds. That's easy when you're Tiger Woods and have thousands of spectators watching your every move. Woods deputized about a dozen muscle-bound followers to roll away the boulder, giving him a clear shot. Woods hit his second into a green-side bunker, blasted out to five feet and sank the putt for birdie. He finished in sole position of third place behind Rocco Mediate and Justin Leonard.

Not surprisingly, the following year the USGA issued a decision prohibiting a player from recruiting assistance for the purpose of moving large loose impediments.

Perhaps because of his consistently excellent play, lefthander Phil Mickelson seems to be involved in a number of rules decisions. In the third round of the 2001 NEC Invitational, Mickelson was playing with leader Jim Furyk when they arrived on the tee of the par-5 16th hole. Mickelson pushed his tee shot way left into an area not used by the gallery. Fortunately for Phil the flight of the ball was followed by the MetLife blimp. With the help of the marshal and television, Phil located a ball that he thought was his. Now he had to mark and lift the ball in order to positively identify it. But he was unsure that the ball was his because it did not have his usual mark. He had put a new ball into play at the beginning of the hole but apparently neither he nor his caddy had put a mark on the ball. At this juncture the miracle of modern television with the ability of instant replay was able to ascertain that the ball he found was undoubtedly his.

From here Mickelson finished the hole registering what he thought was a bogey-six. But wait! Even though he was positive that the unmarked ball was his, he had failed to explicitly inform his fellow-competitor that he was going to mark and move his ball for the purpose of identification. Despite the fact that he had been heard by a vast television audience, he had failed to tell Furyk. Rule 12.2, which deals with identifying your ball, now came into play. It states "except in a hazard, the player may, without penalty, lift a ball he believes to be his own for the purpose of identification and clean it to the extent necessary for identification. Before lifting the ball, the player must announce his intention to his fellow-competitor."

"Unfortunately, when I marked it to identify it, I vocalized my intentions, but I didn't vocalize toward Jim," said Mickelson.

Mickelson was assessed a one-stroke penalty and recorded a seven for the hole.

This tournament seems to have been beset by this particular rules violation. Kirk Triplett also became a casualty. In Saturday's third round Triplett had occasion to mark his ball and lift it for purposes of identification. He, too, failed to notify his playing partner, Lee Westwood, of his intentions. During the front nine of his final round Triplett became aware of Mickelson's mistake. He reported his own situation to an official on the 10th tee. Since the accompanying one-stroke penalty had not been included on Saturday's scorecard, he was disqualified. Nevertheless, he received unofficial last-place money of $26,000.

The following case demonstrates one of the few differences between the rules of golf as presented by the USGA and the R&A. While it's a small detail, foreign players and those who travel the world to make their living playing golf must be aware of the difference.

During the third round of the 1999 Masters, Ernie Els' tee shot on the par-3 16th came to rest directly behind a large sprinkler, just a foot or so off the green. The South African asked for a ruling, unsure if he was entitled to relief from the sprinkler. Els' confusion stemmed from the fact that the R&A allows a local rule permitting the player to drop the ball to one side if the sprinkler is on a direct line to the hole, provided the sprinkler is within two club-lengths of the green and the ball is within two club-lengths of the sprinkler head. The USGA grants relief only if the sprinkler head interferes with the player's stance or swing.

The R&A's position is based on the fact that on the links courses of Scotland and England the green and the fringe often blend together. Quite frequently players will use a putter from a great distance off the green. In the United States courses are manicured differently, often having rough within two or three feet of the surface of the green. The USGA's concern is that relief from a sprinkler head directly on a player's line might lead to creative interpretation, taking a player from the rough to the fringe.

It is important to note that both the USGA and the R&A allow a player relief if both the obstruction and the ball are on the green.

For the record, Els did not receive relief from the sprinkler head.

The Masters is a tournament unto itself. It's in its own league and does its own thing. There can be little, if any, debate that it is the best-organized tournament in the world. The Masters does things the way the Masters Committee deems them to be done—no discussion, no debate. This occasionally pertains to the rules. In the past it applied the rules the way it saw fit. This was never more evident than two incidents involving Arnold Palmer. At the time of both incidents, the Masters Committee administered the rules of golf at their tournament and provided their own rules officials. It was not until some years later that the USGA took over this function.

Palmer won the first of his four Masters titles in 1958, but it was not without the help (perhaps) of a most controversial and curious ruling. Palmer began the final round tied with Sam Snead and three shots ahead of Ken Venturi, with whom he was playing. By the time they came to the 12th tee, Snead had faded but Venturi was only one back. Number 12, as almost every golf fan knows, is a short par-3 with a shallow green directly behind Rae's Creek, with a bunker in front of the green and a bunker and steep bank at the rear. Venturi played first and saw his shot hit the rear bank and trickle back down onto the green. Palmer hit almost the exact same shot, but the ball plugged in the bank. Now the question arose. Palmer wanted relief, but rules official Arthur Lacey said no, basing his decision on a pronouncement by the Masters Committee earlier in the day. His understanding of the decision was that a player was allowed relief from an embedded ball only on the greens and fairways. Palmer protested, believing that he should be afforded relief anywhere on the course (except hazards, of course).

In the interest of time, Palmer was allowed to play two balls—one from the embedded lie and a second ball from the bank with relief from the embedded situation. Arnold made five with the first and par with the second. With Venturi making par, the leader situation was confused.

Going up 13 the group was approached by Bill Kerr, an assistant to Clifford Roberts, the Masters dictator. Kerr had gotten wind of the incident and wanted details. Kerr agreed with Palmer and gave an "unofficial" ruling that Palmer's three on number 12 would stand as the score. In the midst of all this, Palmer eagled the par-5 13th and Venturi birdied. So now, at least unofficially, Palmer was two shots ahead of Venturi.

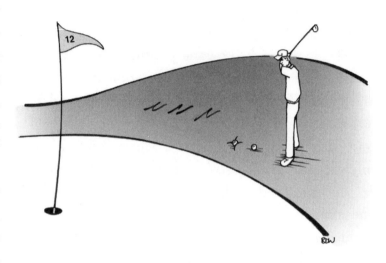

When they reached the 14th tee, Bobby Jones and Clifford Roberts arrived and a group huddle ensued. Jones and Roberts then made it official: Palmer had made a three on number 12. All this finally unnerved Venturi and he three-putted 14 and 15. In the end Palmer won by one over Doug Ford and Fred Hawkins. Venturi finished fourth, two shots behind Palmer.

Did Palmer get a call normally reserved for the home team? Yes? No? Undecided? Well, consider this.

Within a few years Palmer got another favorable ruling. During the tournament, Palmer mishit an explosion shot from a greenside bunker on number two with the ball remaining in the bunker. Palmer angrily slammed his club into the sand. Jack Tuthill, the rules official with the group, called a two-stroke penalty on Palmer for grounding his club in a hazard. But it was not long before the Masters Committee overruled Tuthill, claiming that Palmer did not intend to improve his lie or test the condition of the sand. Even the USGA was talked into agreeing with the ruling, albeit after strenuous debate. Fortunately, this incident did not affect the outcome of the tournament (compare this incident to the one involving Thomas Bjorn in the 2003 British Open. Bjorn's actions were not looked at so generously).

Now contrast these two incidents with the Roberto de Vicenzo scorecard fiasco in 1968 (see the chapter on The Scorecard). In that case, the Masters Committee held fast to the rulebook.

A similar incident befell Scott Dunlap in the 1999 Dimension Data Pro-Am. Dunlap came to the final hole with a five-shot lead, but landed his approach shot in a bunker adjacent to the green. His first play from the bunker only moved the ball 10 yards and it remained in the bunker. Nevertheless, his caddy began to rake the area from where he played his first shot. The rules official on the scene called a two-shot penalty, believing that Rule 13.4 should be invoked. However, before Dunlap could sign his scorecard, tournament director Theo Manyama telephoned the R&A to validate the penalty. The penalty invoked by the rules official was reversed, citing the fact that since the ball was 10 yards away from the original bunker shot, the act of raking the bunker had no effect on the playing of the next shot.

———

You would logically think that virtually identical situations would have similar interpretive results. Rules officials working the numerous professional golf tours around the world have essentially identical rulebooks. It is reasonable thinking, but not necessarily correct. Interpretations may differ 180 degrees. The rules of the game and the decisions that have followed can be so involved that even the most experienced rules officials will come to different conclusions. Here are two situations that for the most part were identical yet were interpreted with opposite results.

The two incidents involve situations from the PGA Tour and the LPGA Tour. Both are interpreted by Rule 13.2, which states that "a player shall not improve…his line of play or a reasonable extension of that line beyond the hole by…creating or eliminating irregularities of surface." In each situation it was the infamous television replay that led to the final decision. Should that produce similar decisions? Not necessarily. In the end they had totally different rulings.

During the 2003 Capital Open at the Avenel TPC just outside Washington, D.C., Duffy Waldorf was involved in struggle for the tournament championship on the final day of play. When he arrived at his tee shot in the fairway of the 12th hole, a difficult dogleg left, he was just three shots out of the lead held by Rory Sabatini. As he was about to play his approach shot, the noise of a golf cart caught his attention and he backed away. But as he reset for his shot, he nervously tapped down a rough patch of grass to the front and right of his ball. Waldorf parred the hole and proceeded to eagle the 13th and birdie the 15th to close to within two shots of the lead, or so he thought. In the middle of the 16th fairway Waldorf was informed by tournament officials that he might be facing a two-shot penalty for his actions in the 12th fairway. An armchair television rules aficionado had telephoned the USGA, expressing his concern over the possibility of a rules violation. The USGA then notified the proper authorities at the tournament site, who cited Rule 13.2. Understandably rattled by the situation, Waldorf bogeyed two of his last three holes.

Before signing his scorecard, Waldorf was permitted to plead his case with head tournament rules official Mark Russell. Waldorf claimed there was no intent to violate a rule. "If I had read the rule, I don't think it would have mattered, because I don't think I was breaking the rule...I told them that if

I hit it directly over the mark I would have hit it 50 yards right of the green."

All that was to no avail. After review by four separate officials, Mark Russell assessed Waldorf a two-stroke penalty, dropping him into a three-way tie for second place and costing him $150,000. "We looked at every way we could to get Duffy out of this," Russell said. "But looking at the [television replay], he physically stepped up and eliminated the irregularity in front of his ball. We just didn't see any way we could get him out of it."

Oh really? No choice but to assess the required two-shot penalty?

Now consider a similar situation that occurred during the 2003 Samsung World Championship, a year-end LPGA tournament with a limited field. Sophie Gustafson began the final day of the Championship five shots out of the lead. However, with a burst of brilliant golf at the beginning of her round, seven under for her first seven holes, she had overtaken the leaders. Then came the incident on the 14th green when her ball moved after she had apparently addressed it (see On the Green, page 158 for an account and assessment of that incident).

While reviewing the replay in consideration of the events on the 14th green, officials noticed that Sophie had tapped down a pitch mark to the front and left of her ball as she was preparing to hit a chip on the very next hole. That could possibly be a violation of Rule 13.2, the same one for which Waldorf was penalized. So everyone, including players, caddies, officials and a few onlookers, hopped into golf carts and scooted out to the 15th green to recreate the situation. After a demonstration by Gustafson and a conference by LPGA officials, it was determined that no violation had occurred. "She did not improve her line of play on the 15th hole," said Charlie Williams, another LPGA Tour rules official.

There are also a couple of intriguing human interest lines involved with these two incidents. In both cases the medium of television was the primary determining element in the eventual decision. In the Waldorf case the whole incident might have gone unnoticed were it not for an armchair rules official. Sitting comfortably at home, he observed Waldorf tap down the patch of grass and called the USGA, who in turn called the PGA Tour to inform them of the probability of a violation. Then the instant replays set in. It's interesting to note that PGA Tour officials had the same view of the incident as did the home viewer. In the end, the Tour agreed with a viewer hundreds of miles away rather than the player and any other eye witnesses who were on the actual spot of the incident. For Gustafson, both incidents were resolved by repeated viewing of the videotape.

Adding more intrigue to the Gustafson situation is the fact that Sophie is the significant other of LPGA Tour Commissioner Ty Votaw. LPGA rules officials and Mr. Votaw have clearly stated that this fact did not exert any influence on their decision in the Gustafson case. Based on Ms. Gustafson's actions this would appear to be an accurate statement.

To conclude this chapter and to illustrate that the job of being a rules official has never been easy, we present two cases from the first half of the twentieth century. The rules may have been a bit different or at least read differently, but the task of interpreting them during the heat of competition has remained the same—difficult and often controversial.

The first involves an interesting interpretation or decision by USGA officials in the qualifier for the 1947 U.S. Open. At that time USGA rules and PGA tournament rules differed in their acceptance of cleaning the ball once it was on the green. The PGA said okay, the USGA, no way. As a result South African Bobby Locke and a majority of the field (about 70%) were granted immunity from this rule since all had operated under PGA tournament rules. USGA officials decided that since the majority had done it, immunity would be granted. By all rights, they should all have been disqualified. History does not record what the other 30% had to say about the matter. One wonders where the principle of fairness and equity come into play here.

In his quest for the Grand Slam in 1930, Bobby Jones became the recipient of one of the most generous rulings in U.S. Open history. Coming to the 71st hole, a treacherous 262-yard par-3, Jones was three shots in the lead. Swinging with all his strength, his tee shot went almost dead right, flying a bunker, hitting a tree, never to be seen again. It may have perished into a swampy area, but no one saw it. Enter USGA referee Prescott Bush. "The ball went into the parallel water hazard," ruled Bush. "You are permitted to drop a ball in the fairway opposite the point where the ball crossed the margin of the hazard." Bobby did. He made double-bogey five and went on to win by two strokes.

Controversial? Yes, sir! That area had not been officially declared a water hazard. Plus, no one actually saw the ball go into the hazard and almost undoubtedly it should have been declared lost. A lost ball would have returned Jones to the tee to hit his third shot instead of playing it from near the green with a relatively easy pitch shot (at least easier than the tee shot). Naturally, the ruling stood.

FOLLOWING THE RULES TO A TEE

If golf distinguishes itself by the honesty and integrity of its participants, then one would think that every player would follow every rule during every round. That might be true in a utopian golf society, but it just isn't so on the public courses of America. Fortunately, most of the rules infractions are not intentional or malicious. Playing "preferred" lies or moving the ball out of a gigantic footprint in a bunker is simply done to enhance the player's enjoyment of the game. Besides, when was the last time you witnessed a PGA Tour player having to endure the malady of a footprint in a bunker?

Whether two local club players follow each and every rule to the letter is not ultimately all that important. Besides a rigid adherence to the rules, there is a metaphysical aspect to the game. This is the spirit of the game: the camaraderie of a good playing partner; the commune with nature; and the physical and mental challenge of the game. All of these (and more) provide the enjoyment that a golfer experiences. Without the spirit of the game, there really is no experience. It is just physical exertion.

Most golfers observe the spirit of the game while not necessarily complying with the strictest confines of the rules. Rigid adherence to the rules is left to the professional tours of the world and golf's governing bodies. But, sometimes, even in a valid effort to preserve the integrity of the game, one of golf's governing bodies fails to see the forest because of the trees. In other words, they lose touch with the spirit of the game.

To illustrate this point we have uncovered a couple of cases that do not focus on a specific rule incident or violation, but rather on an organization's approach to the rules.

Before there was Casey Martin, there was Charlie Owens and the 1987 U.S. Senior Open. The USGA ruled that Charlie Owens, like everyone else, was obligated to walk the course during the competition. On the surface that may look like an equitable decision, but there's more to the story than that.

For those of you who are not familiar with Owens' plight, he has numerous lower body ailments that were incurred during a 1952 parachuting accident while he has serving in the Army. His primary ailment is a fused left knee and ankle. The course for the competition, Brooklawn Country Club in Bridgeport, Connecticut, was not long but quite hilly. The USGA "generously" let him use crutches whenever necessary. In valor he completed only nine holes and was forced to withdraw. He could walk no longer.

It is necessary to understand that the USGA considers walking and stamina part of the game. They did prior to 1987, they did in 1987, and they still do now. Therefore, participation in any event conducted by the USGA means that you walk. At least it did until the Casey Martin case. When Martin played in the U.S. Open at the Olympic Club in 1998, he was allowed to use a cart. Of course, there was some serious litigation pending at the time.

But you have to consider what the Senior Tour (now called the Champions Tour) was in 1987 and still is today—a nostalgic exhibition. Back then, as it is today, the seniors were allowed to use carts in regular tour events, which were conducted by the PGA Tour. But at the U.S. Senior Open, then and now, it's no carts.

But what's wrong with letting the seniors use carts if they so desire? The USGA makes other concessions to the seniors that do not involve specific points in the rules. Frank Hannigan, who was a member of the USGA tournament committee at the time of the Charlie Owens situation, stated that the course for the Senior Open was not set up with the same degree of difficulty as the U.S. Open. The fairways are wider; the rough is not as thick and the greens are not as firm and fast. Certain concessions are made; others are discarded. One wonders how the decisions are made. However, these are not rule-governed issues.

———————

Virtually every major organization in golf, whether self-appointed or not, is continually attempting to bring more people into the game, certainly a noble undertaking. But there are times when an organization follows the rules right to the letter and squelches the spirit of the game, even to the point where lawyers need to become involved. Regardless of your opinion of the legal profession, litigation has become an integral part of our society, and with increasing frequency, that has infiltrated the world of golf. Such cases as those involving Casey Martin vs. the PGA Tour and Callaway (and other club manufacturers) vs. the USGA serve as examples.

But even with the high profile cases notwithstanding, the little guy can encounter an interpretation of the rules that requires the services of the legal profession. Consider the following situation.

When Matthew Ross was nine years old, he carried a 27 handicap and he had won a couple of tournaments. But, according to the rules of golf as interpreted by the Greater Tampa Junior Golf Association, Matthew was barred from further competition because of his other handicap. Matthew is autistic and unable to keep an accurate count of the number of shots he has taken. Under Rule 6.6 each competitor is required to keep his own score, or at least record the score of a fellow competitor and check and sign his own scorecard.

Fortunately, when the details of Matthew's situation became public, the reaction was swift and furious. In an attempt to salvage the situation and distance themselves from some ugly exposure, the USGA issued a press release stating that a local committee has the right to waive the applicable principles of Rule 6.6 with a local rule.

The good news is that's exactly what happened. The bad news is that it didn't happen until the Florida State Attorney General's office became involved. It wasn't until an attorney for the Advocacy Center for Persons with Disabilities pressed the GTJGA for a solution that the GTJGA agreed to a compromise. Matthew would be allowed to have a mentor with him on the course. This mentor would be someone trained in interaction for people who have autism.

The board of the GTJGA stated, "...Matthew may have a mentor who meets the criteria outlined in your letter and that he or she may have access to Matthew at all times, before, during and after the tournament play."

Other conditions and stipulations were agreed upon by both parties, but the end result was that Matthew was able to play competitive golf again, one of the joys of his life.

The bigger issue here is that the spirit of the game was upheld. Golf is still just a game and is meant to be fun. Regardless of the monetary considerations that influence the game at the current time, the majority of golf that is played is recreational and should never be affected by litigation.

CONCLUSION

Many of the preceding incidents may have left you shaking your head and asking how a professional golfer could not know that. Many of the scenarios may have touched your sense of humor as you pictured the scene in your mind's eye. And a few of the incidents may have touched your heart as you observed how golf exposes the true character of an individual. But the one conclusion that we can draw from this entire examination is that the rules of golf as published by the USGA and the R&A are central to the game. They are the backbone of a sport that requires physical action based on mental preparation. Regardless of the circumstances, conditions or other mitigating factors, the rules make the game what it is.

If we reflect on the rules, we will discover that they not only provide the structure for how the game is to be played, but also produce the spirit of the game. Just as the two great principles of the game are interwoven throughout the entire rule book, so is the spirit of the game with its demand on each player for honesty and integrity. Golf is the only sport in which players must police their own play. As far as the rules are concerned, each player is responsible for his own conduct on the golf course. The fact that this happens speaks volumes for the spirit of the game.

Within the spirit of the game golf develops positive character traits. This is clearly apparent when we read about Kyle Hitchcock in the final incident in the chapter on Honesty. Hitchcock needed no outside encouragement. Realizing what makes golf the great game that it is, he immediately took the honorable action.

The spirit of the game demands that every player should adhere to the rules regardless of his or her playing ability. Whether one is competing on the national level, local club level or all alone against the golf course, the honesty and integrity of the game must be upheld and the rules must be followed.

It has often been said that golf is a microcosm of life. If we play the game with honesty and integrity, we will walk through life in the same manner.

Golf becomes a reflection of who we really are.

BIBLIOGRAPHY

Dobereiner, Peter. *Golf a la Carte*. New York: Lyons & Burford, 1991.

Marrandette, David G. *Golf Playoffs: A Sourcebook of Major Championship Men's and Women's Amateur and Professional Playoffs, 1876-1990*. Jefferson: McFarland & Company, Inc., 1991.

Murray, Francis. *The British Open: A History of Golf's Greatest Championship*. Chicago: Contemporary Books, Inc., 2000.

Nash, Bruce and Allan Zulo with George White. *The Golf Nut's Book of Amazing Feats & Records*. Chicago: Contemporary Books, Inc., 1994.

Palmer, Arnold with James Dodson. *A Golfer's Life*. New York: Ballantine Books, 1999.

Penick, Harvey with Bud Shrake. *The Wisdom of Harvey Penick*. New York: Simon and Schuster, 1997.

Tufts, Richard S. *The Principles Behind the Rules of Golf*. Far Hills: United States Golf Association, 2000. Reprint of 1960 edition.

The Rules of Golf. Far Hills: The United States Golf Association, 2003.